I Am Persuaded

Propiv Press
Lancaster, Pennsylvania, USA

I Am Persuaded

Christian Leadership
as Taught by Jesus

By Jonathan Brenneman

Foreword by Brian Hogan

I Am Persuaded

Christian Leadership as Taught by Jesus

General Editor Jan C. McLarty

Propiv Press, Lancaster, Pennsylvania, USA

ISBN   13:978-1502775955
        10:1502775956

Printed in the United States of America.

Unless otherwise indicated, Bible quotations are taken from the 1769 King James Version of the Holy Bible, from the free Bible software program, E-Sword (www.esword.net). Other Bible versions used include: Holy Bible, New International Version (NIV), © Copyright 1973, 1978, 1984 by International Bible Society; Young's Literal Translation of the Holy Bible (YLT) by J. N. Young, 1862, 1898; The Weymouth New Testament (WNT) by Richard Francis Weymouth, 1903; International Standard Version (ISV), © Copyright 1995-2014 by ISV Foundation—All Rights Reserved Internationally; Good News Bible (GNB)—Second Edition, © Copyright 1992 by American Bible Society; Literal Translation of the Holy Bible (LITV), © Copyright 1976-2000 by Jay P. Green, Sr. All rights reserved.

I used the free Bible study software E-Sword extensively, from www.e-sword.net (© Copyright 2012—Rick Myers E—Sword Version 10.1.0). It links the KJV to Strong's Concordance so I could find every place in the KJV a certain English word was used and search the Strong's word number for every place a certain Greek word was used. References to meanings of Greek words are from Strong's Hebrew and Greek Dictionaries within the E-Sword program.

Cover art: Arnolda Brenneman
Cover: Grant Visagie

Dedication

I dedicate this work to all those who love the Lord Jesus with an undying love, and to those, past, present, and future, who lay down their lives for God's flock.

What People Are Saying

Those who have spent any time in "organized" Christianity in the West have experienced what Jonathan brings to light: there is a weird and uncomfortable mixing of the teaching of Jesus and the religion people make up about Jesus. Jonathan puts his finger on the most lethal part of that concoction: hierarchy, the rule of the priests/pastors. Jonathan engages in a close reading of Scripture as well as a thoughtful reflection on his experience and role models to refocus us on the centrality of Jesus as our boss and owner. He moreover brings attention to the importance of our loving (and not controlling) relationships with one another as brothers and sisters in the body of Christ.

There is a lot to take in here, but I am left with three urges after reading Jonathan's soulful writing: (1) To remember I am your servant, but you are not my master. Jesus is. (2) To keep finding the Spirit's liberation as we know the truth from a close reading of scripture. (3) To keep going in obedience to Christ, regardless of the approval of people in positions and organizations. I commend this heartfelt reflection of a devoted follower of Jesus to you.

BRIAN DODD—Orlando, Florida. Pastor, 25 years;
Ph. D., University of Sheffield, England, New Testament Studies;
Former Professor: Fuller Theological Seminary,
Asbury Theological Seminary;
Author: Praying Jesus, Where Christology Began, The Problem with Paul,
Paul's Paradigmatic 'I': Personal Example as Literary Strategy,
Empowered Church Leadership: Ministry in the Spirit According to Paul.

I commend Jonathan for writing a book which systematically dismantles one of the greatest misconceptions in the church today—ecclesiastical authority. The material found within the pages of this motif not only challenges the mindsets of religious traditions of men, but also lays a biblical foundation for true authentic leadership, using Jesus Christ as our model and personal example for leading/serving others.

At a time when progressive truth is breaking forth in many different aspects of the gospel of the kingdom, such as abundant grace, divine healing, and the fullness of who Christ is in every believer, it's no surprise that the Holy Spirit has spoken so clearly through Jonathan in an effort to declare truth in love to the body of Christ concerning godly authority. It's my honor and privilege to endorse this work of progressive truth. I trust, like a clarion sound, it'll provoke change in the hearts of leaders as deep calls out to deep, challenging leaders to change through revealing the simple truths of the gospel.

PAUL GRAVES—Founder, Bible to Life Ministry,
Durban South Africa
Author, "Every Believer's Authority"

I Am Persuaded is a practical, biblical and needed fresh look at ruling, serving, obeying and leadership in the body of Christ. As Christians living in a kingdom that is not of this world, the present hierarchical mindset from the world's system does not fit. The current hierarchical model of leadership will only serve to work against unity and the new covenant expression of the kingdom that is from above. Jonathan has done a great job of giving us a fresh perspective of *greatness* and *serving* that looks like what Jesus himself described and modeled. This is a great resource to help correct the mindset of modern Christianity, so as to function in unity and honor, and to live as a body with One Head.

THOMAS SERSEN—Missionary/Pastor
Abounding Grace Ministries International Church, South Korea.

Jonathan Brenneman in his *I Am Persuaded* provokes, jabs and challenges our sacred cows of church leadership. Yet, the jabs are not hurtful because they come from Scripture. This is not a reactionary book filled with leader bashing but a graceful and excellent presentation of mostly forgotten principles concerning how Jesus and the early church taught and practiced leadership.

All the key and at times controversial words are discussed: rule, obey, submission, apostles, authority, and spiritual covering. Excellent exegesis on these words is provided and is foundational to the author's conclusions. If you find yourself disagreeing, then, by all means, do a better exegesis. I think that will be difficult. Jonathan Brenneman has personally made a *paradigm shift* in his life and shares it with us. Will you?

I Am Persuaded is more than a fine Bible study, it is filled with real life stories which illustrate servant leadership. It is well written, fast paced, and provokes fresh thinking. I believe the reader and the church will be healthier when these principles are put into practice. Will you be persuaded? Will you undergo a paradigm shift? Read and find out. This is a good book and its message needs to be heard.

DR. STAN NEWTON—Missionary in Bulgaria;
Author: Glorious Kingdom.

The issue of authority and submission in the church is like Goldilock's porridge: it's hard to get it just right. There are leaders who treat people like consumable commodities for their drive, ambition and self-perceived Old Covenant Mosaic style of leadership "vision." There are also people who abuse leaders thinking it is their holy mandate to keep them shamefully poor, discouraged, and depressed. It's as if they believe their recalcitrance is ordained by God to keep their leaders "humble." Both are nonsense. Both are abuse. Both are reactionary. Both are unacceptable.

It can be difficult to find a healthy middle road of new covenant mutuality and service in other-ness on this topic. Jonathan Brenneman has made a fine contribution toward this end with this work. Jonathan has discovered, as so many have, that many of the words translated with a hierarchal bias in the English scriptures, are simply not so in the original Greek. Rather, many English translations represent the worldview and bias of the translators. This is especially so of 16th and 17th century translations from monarchial cultures that believed in the divine right of kings and absolute submission to them as equivalent to what should occur in the ekklesia. That is simply bias, not "truth." It does not belong in Christ's kingdom.

Without getting too bogged down in the technical details of language that might lose some readers, Jonathan provides just enough to make his case and to persuade readers to reconsider many things they may have been taught about authority and submission. It gladdens my heart to know younger generation believers are discovering, in their twenties and thirties, what did not come to me until my fifties. This is generational progress worth celebrating! These younger generation believers will be neither snared nor distracted by the ridiculous and biblically unjustifiable leadership doctrines that are so prevalent today, especially in many independent and non-denominational churches. They will not have to deconstruct the influence of decades of various forms of "leadership" doctrinal rubbish, but rather can be free to give themselves to the King and his kingdom.

DR. STEPHEN R. CROSBY—*Stephanos Ministries;*
Author: Authority, Accountability, and the Apostolic Movement;
www.stevecrosby.com, www.stevecrosby.org

Jonathan shares some great observations on leadership in I am Persuaded. If you're looking for fresh insights on church dynamics, this book provides sound ideas for you to consider.

PRAYING MEDIC—http://prayingmedic.com/
Author "Divine Healing Made Simple: Simplifying the supernatural to make healing and miracles a part of your everyday life" and "My Craziest Adventures With God-The Supernatural Journal of a Former Athiest Paramedic"

I am Persuaded is a wonderful read focusing on The Lord's view of true leadership. It was never his desire that we would model ourselves after the kingdoms of this world. This book inspires the reader to lean on the power of the Holy Spirit, taking on a servant's heart which is the essence of true discipleship and leadership. This book reveals the secret to true success in ministry and provokes us as leaders to focus more on leading by example and less on our "positions" in the church.

Thanks Jonathan. May your writings be blessed by the Lord and inspire his church to be more like him.

STEPHEN P. SERSEN— Associate pastor at Maranatha Chapel, Baltimore, Maryland

Foreword

Solomon said that "the writing of many books is endless," and had he lived to glimpse the sheer volume of volumes on the subject of leadership that sags the shelves of pastoral libraries, he would have surely felt he'd understated the matter.

Does the Christian world really need another book on leadership? If we are talking about the kind of books crowding the aforementioned pastoral libraries, then the answer is a resounding "NO." These books tend to endlessly tweak the notions of the nature of leadership already endemic and fully engaged in the Western Church. Church leaders read them and "step up their game" without ever really being challenged to completely change the game they are playing.

The only book on leadership that the world needs is one that points to the *one Book* that really matters—to inspire pulling it out for re-examination (or maybe for many, deep examination for the first time) of the Jesus-style of leadership found there. This leadership can be observed in the way both Jesus and Paul modeled it to the Early Church. If someone were to write a leadership book like that—saturated with applicable Scripture—to challenge our organizational and structured traditions for "ruling" the Church, that would be a book worth writing and reading!

Jonathan Brenneman has produced just such a book in "I Am Persuaded: Christian Leadership as Taught by Jesus." In this book he pulls out, pulls apart, and dissects our cherished assumptions and traditions about leadership in the Church, and he does it all with a surgeon's skill under the bright and penetrating light of New Testament Scripture.

I have been amazed and delighted at the contradictions exposed and fresh insights garnered. Brenneman's book has the potential to calm and bring light to the sea of change that many are experiencing in their journey from institutional to organic expressions of Church life. In that sense it is timely. Every previous reformation has brought great change and purification to doctrine and spiritual practices, but left the structure and hierarchy basically untouched and untroubled in patterns forged under Emperor Constantine seventeen centuries ago.

The ideas in this book, if applied in new wineskins—new structures made for the new wine the Father is pouring out—have the potential to complete the Reformation. That is, what is expressed in *I Am Persuaded* has the potential to free the people of God from domination by a priestly class and re-launch what Jesus gave us: the priesthood of all believers.

I had personal experience in planting the Church in absolutely virgin soil in Outer Mongolia in the early 1990s. *The entire story is in my book*: "There's a Sheep in my Bathtub: Birth of a Mongolian Church Planting Movement." Our church planting team worked very hard to leave the "heavy package" of Westernized institutional church at home and use the New Testament as a filter for practices we introduced among the Mongolians. We were largely successful and were led by the Spirit into a number of the concepts found within Brenneman's book. I would, however, have considered *I Am Persuaded* an absolute treasure had it been available at the time.

One chapter in particular is "worth the price of admission." In *Chapter 2: Three Misleadingly Translated Words*, Brenneman discloses a disturbing and amazingly erroneous word choice by the King James translation team that has blinded us to what Jesus really taught about leadership ever since 1611. The Greek words translated there as "rule over," "rule" and "obey" all clearly mean something else—something that actually agrees with the teachings of Jesus!

In a similarly brilliant manner, Brenneman plows on to demolish the concept that a hierarchy in the Church is envisioned in the New Testament; that is, he begins with and clarifies how we have defined the roles of pastor, bishop, and deacon to imply false ideas of authority, and then goes on to rectify so much more! Brenneman calls on the Church to go back to a trust in the Holy Spirit who has never resigned the job of building and leading his Church. Even sacred cows like the teaching of "Spiritual Fathering" and "Covering" come under his scriptural scalpel with devastating effect. He calls each of us back to more biblical patterns of relating one to another, as opposed to ruling over each other "as the Gentiles do."

This stuff is pure gold! It is potential dynamite to the status quo of church as we know it—exactly the church as we know it that Brenneman urges us to consider "*letting go*" of in order to follow Jesus into Church as God desires it.

Finally, I was greatly stirred and encouraged by what this book has to say about *Youth With A Mission* and its founder, Loren Cunningham. Loren had to put the vision and call God had given him first, even though his spiritual leaders were forbidding Loren's pursuit of what God had spoken.

The result? The fruit of Loren's obedience is the world's largest mission taskforce!

I have personally experienced opposing human authority every time God spoke into my life. In order to push through to the call of God on my life, I had to learn that many of the familiar tenets of submission were just plain sub-biblical. Because I would not take my pastor's "No" as final, Jesus is worshipped today by tens of thousands of Mongolian disciples, plus their disciples in dozens of other nations. I am excited that as you read this important book, you will understand how this book hit home for me.

I am filled with thanks to the Father that he has inspired Jonathan Brenneman to write a book with such incredible promise. It is a book with the potential to not only lead us out of our 1700 year "Babylonian Captivity" to human principles of control, but to point us on into the promised land of family relationship with him and one another in Christ!

Brian Hogan
Serves with Church Planting Coaches
and the Frontier Mission Leadership Team of
Youth With A Mission (YWAM);
Author of "There's a Sheep in my Bathtub:
Birth of a Mongolian Church Planting Movement",
and "An A to Z of Near-Death Adventures"

Preface

After the abuses of the Shepherding Movement in the 1970s, many Christian leaders flinch at the topic of authority and submission, and rightly so! On the other end of the spectrum, there are leaders still writing and espousing false teachings about being "Under Cover," and the concept of "Spiritual Authority" is heralded as a hierarchical structure that God ordained.

Jonathan Brenneman has added wisdom to this confused realm of pain and abuse. He clears the undergrowth of brush and chaos with his refreshing perspective in his book, *I Am Persuaded*. As you take the time to digest this book, allow yourself to see Jesus' leadership style through new eyes.

Jesus knew that the Father had put all things under his power, and that he had come from God and was returning to God (John 13:3). Jesus possessed unlimited power, and he knew it. He also knew where he had come from (identity) and where he was going (purpose). The apostle John tells us Jesus knew his own greatness and the scope of his authority—even before the cross—and in light of these very great realities, he purposefully decided to take the position of a servant. In other words, the power didn't go to his head. It only caused him to bend lower and love more. This is why he got up in the middle of the last supper, took off his outer garments, and wrapped a towel around his waist so he could wash the disciples' feet.

Though Jesus held the most amazing position possible as the all-powerful Son of God, he humbled himself in a very tangible way. Imagine becoming president or king or top leader of the largest nation or entity in the world! Jesus' position far exceeded that. God had given him all power. It is hard to even comprehend the meaning of such a grand declaration. As Jesus stood in that incredible moment, the natural conclusion for him was, "This means I need to wash some feet." It is almost incomprehensible for us, because it falls so far outside our grid for greatness. How in the world does that make any sense?

Really, it should stun us. After all, foot-washing in that day was very different from foot-washing as we know it. It is not too difficult to wash the reasonably clean feet of someone who had a shower in the morning and has worn socks and shoes since. In Jesus' day, foot cleanliness as we know it did not exist. People wore open-toed sandals and walked on dirt roads behind camels in a very warm climate—with the result that foot-washing was a messy job assigned to the lowest slave in the house. It was the lowest of low positions: the one who cleaned dirt and sweat and "camel stuff" off people's feet when they came over.

This is the foot-washing that Jesus did! In this light, when Jesus talked about leadership, He meant that those who are the greatest and have all of the power—those who are the most spiritual and have the greatest anointing and calling—these are they who should willingly take the lowest place of servant-hood in the house. This is how Jesus saw it: "Since God has given me the highest place, I need to take the lowest place." That's what leaders with great authority do: they take the lowest place of service. This is both natural and logical in Christ's Kingdom. Being a great leader means being the foot-washer.

Dr. Jonathan Welton
Best Selling Author & President of Welton Academy

Table of Contents

Introduction
Changes in Perspective

A Child's View of Scripture

I remember when I received my first Bible. My grandmother told me that when I was old enough she would give me one. I think that most young children become eager to get anything that they need to be old enough to have. If a Bible was something that I needed to be a certain age to have, then I wanted a Bible!

When I first began learning to read, I had great difficulty, but when I was almost seven years old, all of a sudden reading became very easy for me, and I became a bookworm. I would sometimes read one or two books every day. So when my grandmother saw how much I loved reading, she gave me a *Good News Bible*. I felt important because I was old enough to have a Bible! I was seven years old.

Whenever I had an interest in something I became intensely focused on it, so I read through the whole thing, although I quickly skipped through some boring parts of Leviticus and First Chronicles. I was still at the age when it is hard to comprehend figurative language, so I did not understand everything well. Psalms, Proverbs, Ephesians, and the teaching of Jesus were my favorite parts of the Bible.

I think that on the one hand, I understood some parts of Scripture better coming from a child's perspective, because I took them for what they said. My view wasn't complicated by complex theological arguments. I simply read things as they were written more easily than an adult might because I didn't have as much tradition to apply to Scripture as many adults would. On the other hand, I was reading a loosely translated, paraphrased version and had no understanding of the historical context in which the Bible was written. Consequently I had many questions, some which were questions many adults did not know how to answer. I noticed things that seemed to be contradictory which I couldn't get a clear understanding about. I think most adults who knew me at that time didn't realize the questions I pondered.

Church Leaders

One of the topics confusing to me concerned submission and authority. When I read the Bible it was pretty clear that I was supposed to submit to my parents, but I was unsure if the Bible taught us to submit to religious leaders. Jesus and Paul seemed to go very much against the religious leaders of their times. I read about honoring *elders*, but I also read about how the elders of Jesus day opposed him, and that Jesus obeyed God whether they liked it or not. Sometimes Jesus spoke very bluntly to these leaders. I read about how Jesus taught his disciples that they were not supposed to rule over each other like the gentiles do, but I also read Hebrews 13:17:

> *Obey them that have the rule over you, and submit yourselves: for they watch for your souls, as they that must give account, that they may do it with joy, and not with grief: for that is unprofitable for you.*

How did these Scriptures fit together? I wasn't sure. I didn't have a logical explanation. However as I grew up, the teaching that I heard in church tended to emphasize Scriptures like Hebrews 13:17, so over time I tended to pay less attention to the words of Jesus.

As a teenager I was very involved in church, and became increasingly involved in different churches in various places. I learned Spanish and visited Hispanic congregations as well as English ones. I wanted to live my whole life for the Lord and felt that I was called to be a missionary. I sometimes went to a church meeting almost every day. There were some things in this that were very beneficial to me, but others that were frustrating or confusing. There were some things that religion taught me that really hurt me, which I later had to unlearn.

I started to go on mission trips when I was a young teenager, and my first trip alone was to Central America when I was 18 years old. The church youth group had been a big part of my life, and as I became a young adult, I stayed on as one of the youth group leaders instead of leaving when I graduated from high school.

The Holy Spirit had already put a great love for people in my heart along with a desire to preach. By now I was very familiar with the Bible, but it was still difficult for me to communicate what I understood as well as I wanted to. I did however begin to get the opportunities to preach at a few different places, including on the radio in Central America!

Increasing Involvement in the Body of Christ

When I was twenty-one, I had a very powerful experience with the Lord that greatly deepened my love for others and enabled me to be a greater blessing to them. I began to spend a lot of time with people, sharing the gospel and praying for them, so that talking to people about Christ became more and more natural for me.

In the next years I made friends with several pastors and had opportunities to exhort, encourage, and pray for believers in several different states and countries. I became involved in a wide variety of Christian groups. My whole desire was to be driven and moved by the love of God, and to serve and bless others. Sharing truth with people and seeing what the Holy Spirit consequently did in their lives was thrilling to me.

As I became more and more involved in the body of Christ in different groups, cultures, and contexts, my desire grew to better understand what the biblical role of a leader in the body of Christ was. I was especially concerned because my heart's desire was to bring the gospel to places where others had not gone, so I needed to know how to lay a foundation.

As the Holy Spirit worked greatly in my heart and increased my love for others, I realized that I seemed to have no peace about doing some things the way that I once thought was the acceptable way to do them. I had many questions.

I saw how things were done in the church in different places and cultural contexts, and I tried to learn from others who seemed to be effective in ministry. I looked for the strengths and weaknesses of different paradigms for leadership. I looked at the way certain Scriptures were frequently interpreted in my culture, and considered if I would interpret them the same way if I was a simple child reading them, or a person from a very different culture. I tried to learn more about the culture in which the Bible was written.

I learned much from missionary church planters who had been quite effective in other parts of the world. Some of them talked about stripping our understanding of how church is to function down to the biblical basics, so as to not impose on another culture the things that Western culture had added to it. I paid attention to what different people more educated than I in biblical languages taught, and I compared different viewpoints. I liked to study by finding what Greek word was used in a passage and then searching to find every other place that it was used in the New Testament. I was often blessed by what I found as I studied in this way.

I began to look more closely at Scripture passages that seemed to be contradictory. I would find out what they said in the original language and identify where the same Greek words were used in other parts of the New Testament but translated differently. I was amazed at what I found! The understanding that I was coming to was a lot different than what I had understood by just reading an English translation of the Greek and Hebrew.

I began to see that the rest of the New Testament was consistent with the teaching of Jesus in the gospels. Over the course of several years, a paradigm shift occurred in my understanding of how Scripture taught that the body of Christ was intended to function.

Non-Hierarchical Paradigm for Christian Leadership

I started discussing these things with different people and discussion groups, and as I conveyed my thoughts and understanding, I was asked by some people to put them into book form. Since I already had a great desire to share what I'd found with others who had questions similar to mine, I decided to do so.

Since many books have been written about leadership, and much has been said about different ministry functions, my purpose is not to cover the whole topic of ecclesiology, rather it is to present my perspective on how leaders in the body of Christ are to lead and how they are to relate to one another. It is also to deal with difficult questions about authority and submission, as well as to show how Scriptures concerning these—that seem on surface level and in English to be contradictory—may be understood in a coherent way. My purpose is to present viewpoints and insights that in my experience many people have not yet heard or considered.

As we continue, there might be some ideas quite new or different for you, and perhaps some you do not agree with; however, my expectation is that any reader hungry for truth will find treasure and rich scriptural insights here, whether fully agreeing with me or not. Please understand that I am expressing many truths that are held in tension as I examine where the balance lies. Even Scripture itself expresses many of these truths in seemingly paradoxical ways.

You will in fact see several paradoxes on these pages. I have certainly tried to deal with this subject as honestly as I can, while making every effort not to twist Scripture to simply make it say what I would like it to say. Neither do I want to avoid anything that Scripture says, but instead comprehend as well as possible what the Scriptures as a whole convey. What follows is the understanding that I have come to.

I hope that what I have to share will be a blessing to others who are also seeking to know how to best serve the body of Christ. It is certainly my intention to help others clear up confusion in the same areas where I was once confused in order to recognize and avoid some of the pits we tend to fall into along the way. We want to avoid error that comes out of reaction to error so as not to fall into the ditch on either side of the road of truth.

Isaiah 30:21

And your ears shall hear a word behind you, saying, This is the way, walk in it, when you go right, or when you go left.

Chapter 1
Foundational Teaching on Leadership Among Us

Building Understanding On the Teachings of Jesus

Scripture teaches that the church is *"built on the foundation of the apostles and prophets, with Jesus Christ as the chief cornerstone"* (Eph. 2:20). It seems reasonable to me to think that this characteristic of being foundational also applies to the teaching of the apostles, prophets, and Jesus. I therefore believe that Jesus' teachings are foundational, with the apostolic teachings in the epistles foundational to a lesser degree while building on the teachings of Jesus in the gospels.

The apostle Peter wrote about the apostle Paul saying, *"His letters contain some things that are hard to understand, which ignorant and unstable people distort, as they do the other Scriptures, to their own destruction."* (2 Pet. 3:16, NIV). Peter was saying that some of Paul's teaching could be easily misused or wrongly interpreted. Therefore, if it seems like part of Paul's teaching in the epistles is contradicting the teaching of Jesus in the gospels, a good approach is to start with the teaching of Christ and then build on it with the teaching of Paul.

Words can often have a certain meaning in one context that they don't have in another. Therefore, it is important to understand that the teaching of Jesus gives a background and context to the teaching of the apostles who walked with him, because the apostles built on what they learned from Christ. All too often I hear an interpretation of something that Paul taught that is based on reading ideas into his teaching that come from a contemporary cultural paradigm rather than from the context of Jesus' words and teaching. This can lead to an interpretation that contradicts the words of Jesus or other Scriptures!

Jesus said in John 3:12, "*I have spoken to you of earthly things and you did not understand. How will you understand if I speak to you of heavenly things?*" We must understand that the way heavenly things work is often different then the way earthly things work. The kingdom of heaven does not function in the same ways as an earthly kingdom does. If we do not start with the teaching of Jesus and take into consideration the whole of Scripture, we may selectively interpret a few Scriptures based on an earthly understanding.

So I am beginning with two passages of Jesus' teaching in the New Testament that I believe are fundamental to understanding the roles of leaders in the body of Christ. Jesus tears down our worldly ideas of how things work and teaches us that in his kingdom, it is different. This is where we need to start.

Matthew 19:30

But many that are first shall be last; and the last shall be first.

Luke 22:24-27

And there was also a strife among them, which of them should be accounted the greatest. And he said unto them, The kings of the Gentiles exercise lordship over them; and they that exercise authority upon them are called benefactors. But ye shall not be so: but he that is greatest among you, let him be as the younger; and he that is chief as he that doth serve. For whether is greater, he that sitteth

at meat, or he that serveth? Is not he that sitteth at meat?
But I am among you as he that serveth.

What so impressed me about Jesus' teaching when I was a child was how radically different it was! I was just eleven-years old and I couldn't stop thinking of Jesus' words like *"bless those who curse you and pray for those who despitefully use you"* (Matt. 5:44). Jesus gave us heavenly wisdom that so often turned natural ways of thinking upside down! In the Matthew and Luke passages about leadership and greatness among us, Jesus is changing the way we think. He shows us that the way the kingdom of heaven functions is radically different then the way an earthly government functions.

Sometimes the words of Christ in Luke 22 (also in Matthew 20:25-28) are thought of as saying that the kings of the gentiles are overbearing, too strict, and abuse authority over others, which we shouldn't do. But what Jesus actually said was simply that the kings of the gentiles exercise lordship and authority over others, yet this *holding authority over one another* should not be so among us. Position in Christ's kingdom is not position over other people but *among them as servants.* The way the kingdom of heaven works is sharply contrasted with the way earthly kingdoms are run.

Leaders Among Christ's Disciples Not To Be Kings

In 1 Samuel 8 we read the story of how the Israelites begged God for a king. God warned that a king would make slaves of them and oppress them by taking tithes and heavy taxes. The people nevertheless insisted on a king, *"that we may be like all the nations"* (1 Sam. 8:20). So the Lord gave them a king but said that by demanding a king as the other nations had, the people were rejecting him as King!

We are not called to be like other nations. We are described as a peculiar people. It is important to note this contrast. We hear much teaching today about leadership in the body of Christ modeled after the way a government of an earthly nation functions, yet Jesus taught that the way they lead is not to be the way we function.

Jesus said that he who is greatest among us should be as one who is younger. The word here "greatest" means "elder." The elders among us are to be teachable and willing to learn from a younger brother as if they were the younger ones! We give preference to elders, but among us it is the elder who should give preference to others as if he were the younger. We actually all should prefer and honor each other, but elders should be best at it as an example for all! We must all become like little children to enter the kingdom of heaven—kingdom meaning reign or rule of heaven, the actual way heaven operates.

Matthew 23:8-12(Good News Bible)

You must not be called 'Teacher,' because you are all equal and have only one Teacher. And you must not call anyone here on earth 'Father,' because you have only the one Father in heaven. Nor should you be called 'Leader,' because your one and only leader is the Messiah. The greatest one among you must be your servant. Whoever makes himself great will be humbled, and whoever humbles himself will be made great.

Again, we see in Matthew 23 that Jesus is laying a foundation in our understanding of how to relate to each other as the body of Christ. Many people avoid the very words of Christ because they don't fit in their current understanding. They will say, *"Well, don't you call your dad 'Father?'"* almost as if to say that Jesus' words were unreasonable, implying that since they don't make cultural sense we should dismiss them. Well, of course I call my earthly dad my father! But why did Jesus tell us to call no man on earth our father? What did He mean?

It sometimes seems that this is one of the most avoided passages when we talk about the roles of men as leaders in the body of Christ. Yet it is one of the most important! I think it should be clear that Jesus is warning us about putting men in God's role. Only God should be the one who primarily fills the role of being our Father, our Teacher, and our Guide. We should never look to one man to fill any of these roles for us! We are all brothers and students!

In the context of the rest of the New Testament, I think we can easily see that although the Lord gives grace to some among us to teach, it is he himself who is to be our Teacher! Although the Lord uses men to play a part in his fathering of us, he himself is our Father!

Hebrews 8:11

And they shall not teach every man his neighbor, and every man his brother, saying, Know the Lord: for all shall know me, from the least to the greatest.

1 John 2:27

But the anointing which ye have received of him abideth in you, and ye need not that any man teach you: but as the same anointing teacheth you of all things.

Even a teacher in the body of Christ is to have the attitude of being a student when relating to others. We can receive and learn from others, and especially from those who have a God-given gift of teaching. We can have teachers but no man should be our Teacher (singular). This is God's role, and we need to rely on him to teach us!

In John 16:13, Jesus tells us that the Spirit will guide us into all truth. It is the Holy Spirit who is to be the guide of every one of us! Yes, Jesus does give us other shepherds (pastors) as well, but He is the chief Shepherd! We must see that the Lord himself fills the roles of Father, Teacher, and Shepherd (Pastor) toward us first and foremost. Other believers can play a part in the functions of fathering, teaching, and shepherding, but they must never be the primary ones who fill these roles in our lives.

Please notice that Jesus, the greatest apostle in history, never called his followers and disciples his *spiritual sons*! He called them his brothers, mothers, and friends!

Mathew 12:49-50

And having stretched forth his hand toward his disciples, he said, 'Lo, my mother and my brethren! For whoever may do the will of my Father who is in the heavens, he is my brother, and sister, and mother.'

No more do I call you servants, because the servant hath not known what his lord doth, and you I have called friends, because all things that I heard from my Father, I did make known to you.

If we want to imitate Jesus and build on his teaching, we need to pay attention to how He—who is greater than any of us—related to his disciples!

Heidi's Story

The book of Hebrews says that we are to pay attention to those who have gone before us and to imitate their faith. I like to look for how believers who have gone before me have practically demonstrated qualities that are worth imitating.

A few people have been examples to me personally of an attitude of teach-ability and humility. I love to talk to older believers and hear how the Lord has worked in their lives. I recently heard an older man whom I admire sharing that the Lord had to correct him through some of the young men he is in relationship with. We need to be careful that—no matter how long we have been believers—we don't lose our ability to relate in the body of Christ as brothers who are learning together.

One of the most highly respected leaders I can think of in the body of Christ today, whom I admire greatly, is a missionary named Heidi Baker.[1] Heidi and her husband Rolland have repeatedly faced incredible difficulties and impossible circumstances in seeking to obey the Holy Spirit and bring the gospel and the love of God to others. They have risked their lives and laid themselves down for the cause of Christ.

The Lord has worked through Heidi and Rolland (and many others who have worked with them) to feed the hungry and to adopt thousands of orphaned children. Whole villages that had never heard the gospel have turned to Christ and thousands of churches have been planted in what many have said is the greatest church-planting movement in history.

Before seeing so much fruit in Mozambique, Heidi and Rolland had been missionaries in other locations for many years where they planted churches. But Heidi was at the end of her rope. She was burnt out and desperately needed God to touch her if she was going to be able to keep going. She heard about God's manifest presence at a church in Toronto and flew there seeking a touch from the Lord.

The Lord met her there and spoke to her through prophesy about giving her Mozambique. He touched her with his power in a very supernatural way, convincing her that he would empower her to persevere and do through his grace what was humanly impossible.

Heidi Baker shares that in Toronto the Holy Spirit repeatedly picked her up, set her on her head, and dropped her. She says that God was telling her that He was turning upside down her whole

---

[1] You can find out more about Heidi and Rolland Baker at their ministry website, IRIS Global, https://www.irisglobal.org/ Although what I have shared is based on hearing Heidi preach several times, much of Heidi and Rolland's story is found in their books at http://www.amazon.com/Heidi-Baker/e/B001JP8H7S/ref=sr_tc_2_0?qid=1433795475&sr=8-2-ent

idea of what it meant to be an apostle. Apostleship did not mean being on top, but being on the bottom! Her understanding of apostleship needed to be turned upside down.

At the Toronto gathering when Randy Clark prophesied to Heidi that God would give her Mozambique, Randy said that the blind would see, the lame walk, the deaf hear, and the dead be raised. Heidi says that after this she started praying for every blind person she came across even though, for a long period of time, none of them were healed. Then the first three blind people who were healed in Mozambique had her name, "Heidi." God told her that this was a sign, because *she* was still blind, but He was opening her eyes!

God was opening Heidi's eyes to see Jesus in those who were considered the lowliest people around her. Seeing Christ in "the least of these" is now a key point of the message that she shares. Heidi says that the street children were her teachers! God taught her that she needed to learn from them, so she took the attitude of a student.

I would like to challenge others who know Heidi's story and recognize the grace of God in her life to consider the lessons that she needed to learn. Before reaping so much fruit in Mozambique, Heidi had already been in ministry for many years, sacrificed everything, and preached to thousands. She had already been involved in revival in Indonesia, and had been a part of many miracles and salvations—*yet she still needed to have her understanding of apostleship turned upside down.* She was still blind. She still needed to learn humility. She needed to learn to let dirty street children in a third world country teach her important lessons.

Could it possibly be that even we who have been in ministry for many years, have seen God move, and have seen miracles, signs and wonders, may still be blind? Jesus' disciples had already gone out and preached the message, healing the sick and casting out demons, but their understanding of what it meant to be great among Christ's disciples was still confused. Could it be that our understanding of apostleship or greatness is still wrong side up? Might we still be blind, without the humility or teach-ability to see Jesus in the smallest, youngest, and most unimpressive of people so as to learn from them?

Chapter 2
Three Misleadingly Translated Words

Seeming Contradictions

Right away when we consider the words of Jesus in the gospels, many questions may come to mind, especially if we have read other parts of the New Testament. There are other Scriptures that can seem quite irreconcilable with the teachings of Jesus.

I have struggled with these questions as many have, and have spent a lot of time seeking understanding of truth that would reconcile the seeming contradictions of these Scriptures. As I dug deeper, searching for the Greek words behind the English translations, I was surprised several times by what I found. It seemed that the English translations of certain passages were sometimes very misleading. My study has led me to conclude that what at first seemed like contrasting teaching in the Epistles is quite consistent with the teaching of Christ.

Here for instance are three words that are translated in certain contexts in a way that seemed to me quite inconsistent with what I found to be their literal Greek meanings and with the ways they are used in other contexts. I will also address several words used in Greek that relate to types of authority or government and the contexts in which they are used in Scripture. The English translations of the Greek words we are discussing are underlined.

Hegeomai

Hebrews 13:7

Remember them which have the <u>rule over</u> you, who have spoken unto you the word of God: whose faith follow, considering the end of their conversation.

Are leaders rulers? If so, why did God say in 1 Samuel 8:7 that by seeking a human king his people were rejecting him as the one reigning over them? Is this verse in Hebrews contradicting the teaching of Jesus who told his disciples that they were not to exercise lordship over others? Is it contradicting the apostle Peter who commanded elders to lead not as lords over the flock but as examples to them?[2]

The underlined word which is translated "rule over," is the Greek word "hegeomai." I searched for and read every place this word is used in the New Testament. There are a few times this word is translated as "governor." Yet it is often translated in other ways as well. There are certainly many uses in which it has no connotation of ruling. It is most commonly used in the sense of saying *to think, consider,* or *esteem.* The following Scriptures are examples of this and in them the underlined word is how "hegeomai" was translated.

2 Corinthians 9:5

Therefore I <u>thought</u> it necessary to exhort the brethren, that they would go before unto you, and make up beforehand your bounty, whereof ye had notice before, that the same might be ready, as a matter of bounty, and not as of covetousness.

---

[2] 1 Peter 5:3

Philippians 3:7
But what things were gain to me, those I <u>counted</u> loss for Christ.

James 1:2
My brethren, <u>count</u> it all joy when ye fall into divers temptations.

Hebrews 11:26
<u>Esteeming</u> the reproach of Christ greater riches than the treasures in Egypt: for he had respect unto the recompense of the reward.

Are people who we esteem or consider honorable sometimes rulers or governors? Yes, they sometimes are. But are they always rulers? No. There are many people we may hold in high regard not because of a position of ruling, but because of their character and example. The word "hegeomai" often does not have the connotation of speaking about a person who is over others. Here are some more uses of the word with the translation of "hegeomai" underlined:

1 Timothy 1:12
And I thank Christ Jesus our Lord, who hath enabled me, for that he <u>counted</u> me faithful, putting me into the ministry.

2 Thessalonians 3:15
Yet <u>count</u> him not as an enemy, but admonish him as a brother.

Philippians 2:3

Let nothing be done through strife or vainglory; but in lowliness of mind let each <u>esteem</u> other better than themselves.

Interestingly, the word "hegeomai" is used to talk about God esteeming Paul as faithful. It is clear that there is no connotation that Paul was over God! The word is used as well in the Philippians example to tell us how we all are to relate to each other. But is it saying we should "rule over" each other? On the contrary, we are to esteem each other better than ourselves!

This word "hegeomai" was also the word Jesus used when he taught about how the working of his kingdom contrasts with the operation of an earthly kingdom:

Luke 22:25-26

And he said unto them, The kings of the Gentiles exercise lordship over them; and they that exercise authority upon them are called benefactors. But ye shall not be so: but he that is greatest among you, let him be as the younger; and he that is <u>chief,</u> as he that doth serve.

The ones who are esteemed among us (this time translated as "chief") are those who *serve*. Might it have been more accurate to translate "hegeomai" as "esteemed" rather than as "chief?" It seems as though the translators translated this word as "rule over" in the Hebrews 13:7 verse because they were coming from a mindset that specifically viewed "rulers" as those who are esteemed in the church.

Remember that at the time the King James Bible (KJV) was translated, leaders in the church had great political power, sometimes more than kings. The translators were viewing this word from the context of the religious system of their day instead of from the context of Jesus' teaching. Translators added the word "over" as it is not found in the original Greek. By contrast, if we compare Scripture with Scripture using the original meaning of words, we see from Jesus' teaching that those who are esteemed among us are servants and not rulers.

The word "hegeomai" is also used in the book of Acts in reference to leaders in the body of Christ where it has been translated as "chief." Let's examine it to get a little more insight into how translations can be misleading.

Act 15:22

Then pleased it the apostles and elders, with the whole church, to send chosen men of their own company to Antioch with Paul and Barnabas; namely, Judas surnamed Barsabas, and Silas, <u>chief</u> men among the brethren.

In the Hebrews 13:7 example, the translators added the word "over" to the translation of the word "hegeomai." It was not in the Greek. Yet here in Acts we see that those who were *esteemed* (translated here again as "chief") in the early church were "among the brethren," not over them. They were not only among the brethren but considered as brothers. They were esteemed not because they were rulers who exercised authority over others but because they were *examples* to everyone.

Proistemi

This word literally means "to stand before." In the KJV Bible it is translated as "rule" several times. However in some more literal translations, such as Young's Literal Translation, it is translated as "lead." Here are some examples of its use in the KJV. The words translated from "proistemi" are underlined.

1Timothy 5:17

Let the elders that <u>rule</u> well be counted worthy of double honour, especially they who labour in the word and doctrine.

Romans 12:8

Or he that exhorteth, on exhortation: he that giveth, let him do it with simplicity; he that <u>ruleth</u>, with diligence; he that sheweth mercy, with cheerfulness.

1Thessalonians 5:12+13

And we beseech you, brethren, to know them which labour among you, and are <u>over</u> you in the Lord, and admonish you; and to esteem (hegeomai) them very highly in love for their work's sake. And be at peace among yourselves.

It is probable that this word "proistemi" was translated in such an authoritarian way because at the time of translation into the KJV, politics and religion were very mixed. "Proistemi" was translated as "rule" because King James required his translators to use the same language traditionally used by the church rather than a literal translation of the Greek.[3] Whether or not this was the case, when we look at uses of the word "proistemi" in other contexts, it becomes clear it was also understood in a very different sense, one corresponding more closely to Jesus' teaching that those who are esteemed among us should be the servants of all.

---

[3] Dr. Laurence M. Vance, *A Brief History of the King James Bible.* Fifteen general rules were advanced for the guidance of the King James translators that included: 3. The Old Ecclesiastical Words to be kept, viz. the Word Church not to be translated Congregation &c. 4. When a Word hath divers Significations, that to be kept which hath been most commonly used by the most of the Ancient Fathers, being agreeable to the Propriety of the Place, and the Analogy of the Faith. Vance Publications, Pensacola, FL. Online: http://www.av1611.org/kjv/kjvhist.html

Chapter 2

Titus 3:8

This is a faithful saying, and these things I will that thou affirm constantly, that they which have believed in God might be careful to <u>maintain</u> good works. These things are good and profitable unto men.

Titus 3:14

And let ours also learn to <u>maintain</u> good works for necessary uses, that they be not unfruitful.

In these verses "proistemi" is also a word describing how we serve. Yes, one who *stands before* (the literal translation) others is sometimes a king or ruler, but not always. The fact that a person stands before others does not necessarily make them a ruler or mean that they even have a position of authority over others. There have been many people in history who were great leaders, but who did not occupy any office. For example Rosa Parks[4] is considered a hero for her stand against segregation, but she had no position of authority. Such people "stand before" others as leaders because they are examples to others.

"Proistemi" is often used in the sense of service. Servants stand before others. We can see this in some of Jesus' parables and accounts of his life. In the culture of that day, those who were eating would recline at the table while a servant would stand before them. When you sit down at a nice restaurant today, a waiter stands before you to wait on you.

As I tried to better understand the word "proistemi," I read a translation of a letter written in Greek in 252 BC by a son to his aging father. The son wrote, *"There will be nothing of more importance for me than to look after you (proistemi) for the*

---

[4] On December 1, 1955, in Montgomery, Alabama, Parks refused to obey a bus driver's order to give up her seat in the colored section to a white passenger after the white section was filled. Online: http://en.wikipedia.org/wiki/Rosa_Parks

remainder of life, in a manner worthy of you, and worthy of me."[5] The son was expressing his love for his father and used "proistemi," saying that he delighted to stand before his aging father. In English this was translated as meaning that he delighted to serve and care for his aging father. Was the son saying that he delighted to rule his father? Of course not!

I also found the word "prostatis," which means "one who stands before." It is the noun form of the verb "proistemi." It is used in Romans 16:2 and translated as "succourer," or "helper." The Young's Literal Translation (YLT) translates it in this same verse as "leader."

Romans 16:1-2

I commend unto you Phebe our sister, which is a servant (diakonos) of the church which is at Cenchrea: That ye receive her in the Lord, as becometh saints, and that ye assist her in whatsoever business she hath need of you: for she hath been a <u>succourer</u> of many, and of myself also.

The word "servant" in verse 1 is "diakonos," which is the word that the English "deacon" comes from. Why was the noun "prostatis" translated here as "succourer" (helper) when the translators interpreted the verb "proistemi" as meaning "ruling" in some other places? Because to translate "stand before" as "to rule" in Romans 16 would indicate Phebe (a deacon) was a ruler of many, including Paul, which the translators would not condone. Phebe, a deacon, ruling over the apostle Paul? Deacons rule over apostles? That of course makes no sense.

A translator coming from the hierarchical mindset that the greatest in the church are rulers perceives the word "to stand before" in the context of elders relating to the churches, and thinks, "In this verse, to stand before others means to rule them." Yet when

---

[5] Moulton, James and George Milligan. *The Vocabulary of the Greek Testament.* Hodder and Stoughton, 1963. London, England: Pg. 551.

he reads the word meaning "one who stands before" in the context of an apostle describing the role of a deacon towards himself and others, and thinks, "In this verse, one who stands before others is one who serves them." This is an obvious inconsistency in translation resulting from reading a certain paradigm back into Scripture that isn't there.

It is true that words may have more than one meaning and can be translated differently in different contexts, but here the difference in translation is based on a mindset that models leadership in the body of Christ after earthly governments, forgetting Jesus' words that it should not be so among us, but whoever would be great must become a servant of all.

Let's contrast the differences between a hierarchical paradigm and the teaching of Jesus. There is a hierarchical paradigm that models leadership in the body of Christ after the leadership of an earthly kingdom. And there is the heavenly paradigm as Jesus taught which He contrasted with earthly wisdom and in which the greatest among us become the servants of all.

Hierarchical Paradigm
Includes the belief that elders are on a higher level than simple disciples and also that deacons are on a lower level than apostles. Therefore in 1 Timothy 5:17 where we read that elders "stand before" (proistemi) the congregation, "to stand before" must mean "to rule." On the other hand, in Romans 16:2 where we read that the deacon Phebe is "one who stands before" the apostle Paul, "one who stands before" must mean "a helper" or "a servant," because a lesser person serves a greater one. This is a paradigm that institutionalizes "respecting of persons," even though Romans 2:11 tells us there is no respect of persons with God.

The Teaching of Jesus
We are on the same level, but those who are esteemed among us lower themselves, in order to support and serve the others. We are all brothers, we are all fellow students, and the greatest among us

25

shall be the servant of all. If Jesus himself is not ashamed to call us friends and brothers, then even the apostle should be able to relate to the youngest disciple as a peer, as to a friend or brother. Jesus taught us to all mutually serve and lay our lives down for each other. Therefore, in 1 Timothy 5:17 where elders "stand before" the congregation, because Jesus said that the greatest among us would be the servant of all, "to stand before" must mean "to help" or "to serve." This then is how we are to understand that the elders who serve well are worthy of double honor: they are esteemed for their maturity and for their humble service.

And in Romans 16:2, we read that the deacon Phebe is "one who stands before" the apostle Paul and others. Since the word "deacon" is simply a Greek word meaning "servant," and "one who stands before" also seems to be a word implying "servant" or "helper," we can understand that Phebe was a servant of Paul and of many others.

If we want to translate "one who stands before" more consistently with the other usage of the KJV, we could translate Romans 16:1-2 as saying that the deacon Phebe was a ruler over the apostle Paul, but to do so destroys any notion that apostleship is a position at the top, with prophets, pastors, deacons, and others underneath. On the contrary, it makes it sound like deaconship must be the top position! An alternative in finding a more consistent translation is to translate "one who stands before" as "a leader" or "an example" thus making Phebe a leader or example to Paul. That is more sensible. To illustrate: if Paul visited Phebe in Cenchrea, Phebe would be a hostess, leader, and example to Paul as she served him and oriented him to her community.

However, it seems that the best translation, in line with the teaching of Jesus and the whole of Scripture, would be to translate "to stand before" as "to serve." The ones who are highly esteemed among us are those who are the greatest servants. Service is mutual. Just as the deacon Phebe served the apostle Paul, the elders also serve the youngest of the disciples.

Peitho

Hebrews 13:17
<u>Obey</u> them that have the rule over (hegeomai) you, and submit yourselves: for they watch for your souls, as they that must give account, that they may do it with joy, and not with grief: for that is unprofitable for you.

Ok, so even though "them that have the rule over you" is really better translated as "those who are esteemed among you," what about the word *obey*? The English word "to obey" implies that the one who is being obeyed has authority to command. But if it is so, then why didn't Jesus obey when the elders of his day wanted people to come on the weekdays to be healed, and not the Sabbath? Why didn't the apostles in the book of Acts obey when they were commanded to no longer preach in the name of Jesus?

I searched for and read every instance of the word "obey" being used in the KJV New Testament, and looked at the different Greek words behind the translations. The Greek uses different language in different contexts but in English we read the same word translated as "obey." It is enlightening when we see how the Greek word used here in Hebrews 13:17 is different from other words more often translated as "to obey" in the New Testament. The lesser used word "peitho," which is translated as "obey" in Hebrews 13:17, means literally "be persuaded by." It is also used in Galations, again translated "obey":

Galations 5:7-8
Ye did run well; who did hinder you that ye should not <u>obey</u> the truth? This <u>persuasion</u> cometh not of him that calleth you.

The noun "persuasion" in Galatians verse 8 is "peismone" (yielding to persuasion, assent) and is derived from the verb "peitho," which was translated as "obey" in verse 7. So although the meaning of the word "peitho" is something similar to the meaning of "to obey," it does not have the same authoritarian tone. W.E. Vine confirms this meaning: "to persuade, to win over, in the Passive and Middle Voices, to be persuaded, to listen to, to obey, is so used with this meaning, in the Middle Voice... The obedience suggested is not by submission to authority, but resulting from persuasion." [6]

A command to "be persuaded by" elders is not at all a command to absolute, unquestioning obedience. Rather it is a command to listen carefully to what they have to say. We are commanded to honor the experience of those who are esteemed among us, and, instead of taking what they have to say lightly, we are to listen carefully to them.

This word "peitho" is only translated a few times as "obey," but it is often translated as "trust," "confidence," or "persuade." Of the fifty-five times that I found it in the New Testament, the KJV only translates it as "obey" or "obeyed" seven times. It is used many times in the context of describing how the apostle Paul spoke to both believers and unbelievers. It is also used in other contexts. In the following verses the underlined word is a translation of "peitho."

Acts 13:43

Now when the congregation was broken up, many of the Jews and religious proselytes followed Paul and Barnabas: who, speaking to them, <u>persuaded</u> them to continue in the grace of God.

---

[6] *An Expository Dictionary of New Testament Words, Vol. 3, p. 124*

Chapter 2

Acts 18:4

And he reasoned in the synagogue every sabbath, and persuaded the Jews and the Greeks.

Acts 19:8

And he went into the synagogue, and spake boldly for the space of three months, disputing and persuading the things concerning the kingdom of God.

Acts 26:28

Then Agrippa said unto Paul, Almost thou persuadest me to be a Christian.

Acts 28:23

And when they had appointed him a day, there came many to him into his lodging; to whom he expounded and testified the kingdom of God, persuading them concerning Jesus, both out of the law of Moses, and out of the prophets, from morning till evening.

2 Corinthians 5:11

Knowing therefore the terror of the Lord, we persuade men; but we are made manifest unto God; and I trust also are made manifest in your consciences.

Acts 5:40

And to him they agreed.

Luke 16:31

And he said unto him, If they hear not Moses and the prophets, neither will they be persuaded, though one rose from the dead.

Romans 15:14

And I myself also am <u>persuaded of</u> you, my brethren, that ye also are full of goodness, filled with all knowledge, able also to admonish one another.

2 Titus 1:12

For the which cause I also suffer these things: nevertheless I am not ashamed: for I know whom I have believed, and <u>am persuaded</u> that he is able to keep that which I have committed unto him against that day.

> *Children obey their parents and servants obey their masters, but disciples are persuaded by those who go before them.*

The word "peitho" is used in our Hebrews 13:17 verse to command the believers concerning how they are to relate to their leaders, and is also used extensively in describing the ministry of the apostle Paul. However it is *never* used in Scripture as commanding obedience to secular authorities or to parents. Instead, other words are used. Here are some Scriptures using the word "obey" in other contexts.

Ephesians 6:1
Children, <u>obey</u> your parents in the Lord: for this is right

Colossians 3:20
Children, <u>obey</u> your parents in all things

Chapter 2

Colossians 3:22

Servants, <u>obey</u> in all things your masters according to the flesh.

1 Peter 3:6

Even as Sara <u>obeyed</u> Abraham, calling him lord.

In the above verses, the underlined words are translated from the Greek word "hupakouo," which means "to hear under." While "peitho" is usually translated in other ways such as "persuade" or "trust," most of the time it is "hupakouo" that is translated as "obey."

The word "hupakouo" is often used in Scripture in speaking of obeying God, obeying the gospel, and obeying truth. It is also the word used to describe the winds, the waves, and evil spirits obeying Jesus' command. But it is never used in commanding disciples to obey their leaders. Rather, in such a case, a word meaning "to be persuaded" is used.

Why the difference? We don't see it in English. When we see more precisely what different words are used and translated as "obey," it seems that the rest of the New Testament is consistent with the distinction that Jesus made between the rulers of the gentiles and those who are leaders among his disciples. Such usage is consistent with the principle that we see in 1 Samuel chapter 8 that God did not want a human leader to be king over his people.

It is very important for us to recognize the distinction between how we relate to Christian leadership and how we relate to parents or secular leadership. The Bible does teach about submitting to abusive and unjust authorities. It teaches servants to submit not only to just masters, but also ones who are harsh. However, I believe it is a big mistake to take the biblical teaching about submitting to unjust authorities out of context and apply it to the way the body of Christ functions.

Not only is the teaching that servants should obey even masters who are harsh and unjust wrongly applied to the context of relating to leaders in the body of Christ, but so is the command for children to obey their parents. The Bible does not teach us to obey religious leaders who are harsh or abusive. Did Jesus? Jesus obeyed his earthly parents even when they didn't fully understand his destiny, and he also obeyed imperfect secular authorities, but he did not obey the hypocritical religious leaders of his day. Rather, he rebuked them and did not hesitate to speak the truth directly.

Contrast with Language Commonly Used in Other Contexts

The New Testament often uses different language when speaking of how believers are to relate to leaders in the church than it uses when speaking of how believers should relate to earthly authorities, whether governments and governors, masters or parents. We do not see much of this difference when reading English translations because different words with differences in meaning are often translated with the same English word. For example, whereas the word "hegeomai" simply means someone who is esteemed (who may or may not be a ruler), there is an authoritarian word that Jesus used to describe how earthly governments "rule." This is the word "archo." It is also used when Romans quotes the book of Isaiah to describe the rule of Jesus.

Again, in the examples that follow, I have underlined the English word translated from the Greek word I am referring to. Here are some uses of the word "archo".

Mark 10:42-43

But Jesus called them to him, and saith unto them, Ye know that they which are accounted to <u>rule over</u> the Gentiles exercise lordship over them; and their great ones exercise authority upon them. But so shall it not be among *you: but whosoever will be great among you, shall be your minister.*

Romans 15:12

And again, Isaiah saith, "There shall be the root of Jesse, and he who is rising to <u>rule</u> nations—upon him shall nations hope."

"Archo" is a word that describes exercising first place in political position. Scripture teaches that Jesus rules (archo), but Jesus prohibited us from ruling (archo) over each other. The related word "arche," meaning "first" in certain contexts is translated as magistrate, power, or principality. Here are four examples:

Luke 12:11

And when they bring you unto the synagogues, and unto <u>magistrates</u>, and powers, take ye no thought how or what thing ye shall answer, or what ye shall say.

Luke 20:20

And they watched him, and sent forth spies, which should feign themselves just men, that they might take hold of his words, that so they might deliver him unto the <u>power</u> and authority of the governor.

1Corinthians 15:24

Then cometh the end, when he shall have delivered up the kingdom to God, even the Father; when he shall have put down all <u>rule</u> and all authority and power.

Titus 3:1

Put them in mind to be subject to <u>principalities</u> and powers, to obey magistrates, to be ready to every good work.

We also have the word "archon" which is translated as "ruler" or "prince." Although it is often used in describing the position of religious leaders among the Jews, it is never used in speaking of leaders among Christ's disciples. I believe that it is a mistake and is unbiblical to try to model leadership in the body of Christ after the leadership of the Jewish nation. The reason God gave us a new covenant was because He found fault with the old one. We are not under the covenant that the Jews were under. The underlined word in the following Scriptures indicate the translation of the word "archon."

Luke 18:18

And a certain <u>ruler</u> asked him, saying, Good Master, what shall I do to inherit eternal life?

John 3:1

There was a man of the Pharisees, named Nicodemus, a <u>ruler</u> of the Jews.

Acts 23:5 "Then said Paul, I wist not, brethren, that he was the high priest: for it is written, Thou shalt not speak evil of the <u>ruler</u> of thy people.

Luke 12:58
When thou goest with thine adversary to the <u>magistrate</u>..."

Romans 13:3

For <u>rulers</u> are not a terror to good works, but to the evil. Wilt thou then not be afraid of the power? do that which is good, and thou shalt have praise of the same.

Matthew 20:25-26
But Jesus called them unto him, and said, Ye know that the <u>princes</u> of the Gentiles exercise dominion over them, and they that are great exercise authority upon them. But it shall not be so among you.

Another related word used is "peitharcheo." You can hear the combination of "peitho" (to be persuaded) and the word "archo," which seems to add a more authoritarian tone to it. Of the four times I found this word used in the New Testament, three times the KJV translates it as "obey."

Acts 5:29
Then Peter and the other apostles answered and said, We ought to <u>obey</u> God rather than men.

Titus 3:1
Put them in mind to be subject to principalities and powers, to <u>obey</u> magistrates, to be ready to every good work.

The word "katakurieuo" means "to exercise lordship over." I found it used four times in the New Testament. Of those four times, three are in the context of prohibiting leaders among the believers from exercising lordship over other disciples.

Mark 10:42-43
But Jesus called them to him, and saith unto them, Ye know that they which are accounted to rule over the Gentiles <u>exercise lordship over</u> them; and their great ones

exercise authority upon them. But so shall it not be among you: but whosoever will be great among you, shall be your minister.

1Peter 5:3

Neither as <u>being lords over</u> God's heritage, but being ensamples to the flock.

Authority

The word "exousia" means "authority." Jesus spoke with authority, and it is clear that his authority came directly from his heavenly Father (which we will talk more about later). Christ gave authority to his disciples to preach the gospel, cast out demons, and heal disease. But he prohibited them from exercising authority over each other as the gentiles do. When believers are commanded to exercise authority in Scripture, it is always authority to do Christ's redemptive work and to speak the truth. It is never to exercise authority over others. The authority to speak the truth and to do Christ's redemptive work is an authority that Christ gave to all believers, not only to leaders.

Following are verses with the word translated from "exousia" listed first as they are used in the context of secular authorities, and then as used in the context of the body of Christ. It appears to me from these examples that the Bible describes people as "authorities" in the context of government positions, but never in the context of referring to leaders in the body of Christ.

Chapter 2

Secular Authorities

Luke 12:11

And when they bring you unto the synagogues, and unto magistrates, and <u>powers</u>, take ye no thought how or what thing ye shall answer, or what ye shall say.

Luke 20:20

And they watched him, and sent forth spies, which should feign themselves just men, that they might take hold of his words, that so they might deliver him unto the power and <u>authority</u> of the governor.

1Corinthians 15:24

Then cometh the end, when he shall have delivered up the kingdom to God, even the Father; when he shall have put down all rule and all <u>authority</u> and power.

Titus 3:1

Put them in mind to be subject to principalities and <u>powers</u>, to obey magistrates, to be ready to every good work.

Romans 13:1-3

Let every soul be subject unto the higher <u>powers</u>. For there is no <u>power</u> but of God: the powers that be are ordained of God. Whosoever therefore resisteth the <u>power</u>, resisteth the ordinance of God: and they that resist shall receive to themselves damnation. For rulers are not a terror to good works, but to the evil. Wilt thou then not be afraid of the <u>power</u> do that which is good, and thou shalt have praise of the same...

The Body of Christ

Matthew 20:25-26

But Jesus called them unto him, and said, Ye know that the princes of the Gentiles exercise dominion over them, and they that are great exercise <u>authority</u> upon them. But it shall not be so among you...

Matthew 10:1

And when he had called unto him his twelve disciples, he gave them <u>power</u> against unclean spirits, to cast them out, and to heal all manner of sickness and all manner of disease.

Luke 10:19

Behold, I give unto you <u>power</u> to tread on serpents and scorpions, and over all the power of the enemy: and nothing shall by any means hurt you.

2Corinthians 10:8

For though I should boast somewhat more of our <u>authority</u>, which the Lord hath given us for edification, and not for your destruction, I should not be ashamed.

Titus 2:15

These things speak, and exhort, and rebuke with all <u>authority</u>. Let no man despise thee.

In these verses we see that Jesus prohibited us from exercising authority over each other, but he gave authority to speak the truth, to tread on the power of the enemy, and to edify people. The word "exousia" is also used in a few places in speaking of an apostle's right to earthly provision. The main place that it is used like this in in 1 Corinthians Chapter 9.

1 Corinthians 9:2-6

If I be not an apostle unto others, yet doubtless I am to you: for the seal of mine apostleship are ye in the Lord. Mine answer to them that do examine me is this, Have we not power to eat and to drink? Have we not power to lead about a sister, a wife, as well as other apostles, and as the brethren of the Lord, and Cephas? Or I only and Barnabas, have not we power to forbear working?

1 Corinthians 9:12

If others be partakers of this power over you, are not we rather? Nevertheless we have not used this power; but suffer all things, lest we should hinder the gospel of Christ.

Here again, the word "over" was added by the translators and is not in the Greek. The Literal Translation of the Holy Bible (LITV) has the word "over" in italics, showing it as a word that was added by the translators but was not in the original text. "Over you" is translated from the genitive case of the word "you." The Strong's concordance number for this word is G5216. Here is the Strong's definition:

humōn, *hoo-mone' Genitive case of G5210; of (from or concerning) you: - ye, you, your (own, -selves).*

Having a word in the genitive case is usually like adding the English preposition "of" before the word. I am familiar with the genitive case as used in Polish and Russian, and it is similar to what the Strong's reference says. In my language studies I learned that the word "genitive" is related to "genesis." So a word in the genitive case often denotes origin. I believe that this passage in Corinthians could either be translated as "authority concerning you" or "authority from (given by) you." Either way, Paul never mentioned authority over individuals, but was speaking specifically of the right of an apostle to receive support.

1 Corinthians 9:18-19

What is my reward then? Verily that, when I preach the gospel, I may make the gospel of Christ without charge, that I abuse not my <u>power</u> in the gospel. For though I be free from all men, yet have I made myself servant unto all, that I might gain the more.

In the above verse we see that Paul was concerned about not abusing this right that he had, so he chose not to use it. Here we see again the truth that greatness in Christ's kingdom is in becoming the servant of all.

I want to repeat here that I believe when we are trying to understand concepts in the New Testament, it is so important to start with the teaching of Jesus. The teaching of the apostles builds on Christ's teaching. It is hard to understand something properly if we do not first have our terms defined. Jesus defined the terms of what leadership among us means. It is true that some words can be defined differently in different contexts. But Jesus has defined what it means to be great, to be first, and to be esteemed among his disciples. When we read of greatness and honor in the rest of the New Testament, we must remember how Jesus defined these things for his disciples.

Of the words we talked about describing secular authorities, several of them were used together when Jesus told us how it should *not* be among us:

Mark 10:42-43

But Jesus called them to him, and saith unto them, Ye know that they which are accounted to <u>rule over</u> (archo) the Gentiles exercise <u>lordship over</u> (katakurieuo) them; and their great ones <u>exercise authority</u> (exousia) upon them. But so shall it not be among you: but whosoever will be great among you, shall be your <u>minister</u> (diakonos).

Matthew 20:25-26

But Jesus called them unto him, and said, Ye know that the <u>princes</u> (archon) of the Gentiles <u>exercise dominion</u> (katakurieuo) over them, and they that are great <u>exercise authority</u> (exousia) upon them. But it shall not be so among you...

So, we see the same words used to describe secular authority and obedience to those authorities are also used by Jesus in teaching about how it should *not* be among us. Leaders among us are not authorized by God to exercise authority over individuals. They are given authority to speak truth and to edify, but not to tear down or oppress people. If leaders in the body of Christ want to speak with authority, that authority must be based on the authority of truth. Authority in the body of Christ is not derived from hierarchical position as is demonstrated in earthly kingdoms.

Instead of using words like "archon" or "ruler," the Bible says that leaders in the Body of Christ are those who are *esteemed* among us (hegeomai), and those who *stand before* us (proistemi). Hegeomai is the same word used by Jesus when he said that those who are esteemed among us will be the servants of all. Proistemi can just as well be a word for service as for leadership. It seems that the teaching of Jesus that the *first will be last and the greatest will be the servant of all* is extended throughout the Epistles in both intent and with the word choices the original writers employed.

41

Out of the four uses in the New Testament of the word "katakurieuo" (meaning "to exercise lordship over"), three are in the context of prohibiting the exercising of lordship over each other among believers. And although leaders among us have authority, it is the same authority that every believer has as given in Christ's commands to us to proclaim truth and to trample on the work of the enemy.

Instead of using the same language that is used when commanding that children are to obey parents, Hebrews 13:17 teaches that we are to "be persuaded by" (peitho) our leaders. The "archeo" which adds a more authoritative tone is left off of "peitho" here. The command is not at all one of unquestioning and unreasoning obedience. Rather the command "be persuaded by" is a command to listen carefully to these people and pay attention to what they have to say. It is telling us not to take their words lightly, but at the same time, the nature of the command "be persuaded by" encourages reason and encourages questions. It encourages us to be like the Bereans:

Acts 17:11

These were more noble than those in Thessalonica, in that they received the word with all readiness of mind, and searched the scriptures daily, whether those things were so.

I conclude that if leaders in the body of Christ are going to speak with authority, that authority must be derived from the authority of truth. It is exercised by influence and example, not by having a worldly sort of kingly authority over others. We are to obey truth, but we are to "be persuaded by" those who have gone before us, searching the Scriptures carefully as the Bereans did to see if what they say is true.

Chapter 3
The Fear of The Lord

The Fear of the Lord is the Beginning of Wisdom

As I have sought to understand the scriptural role of Christian leadership, I have found the truths Scripture teaches about leadership seem to be directly related to the fear of the Lord. Moreover, it is as the Holy Spirit teaches me and helps me to serve others and to speak the truth that I have gained practical understanding of the importance of knowing the fear of the Lord.

The concept of "the fear of the Lord," is common in Scripture, and the phrase is found many times in the books of Psalms and Proverbs. When the Bible says that a person feared the Lord, it is saying that they did what was right and shunned evil. It is an expression of faith in God. A person who feared the Lord was a person who knew that God saw not only their words and actions, but also the intentions of their hearts. To fear the Lord is to care about what God thinks more than about anything else.

Both Psalms and Proverbs say that the fear of the Lord is the beginning of wisdom. In the Book of Job we read not only that the fear of the Lord is the beginning of wisdom, but also that it is wisdom! Since we are discussing the topic of leadership in the body of Christ, and since we need wisdom in this respect, acquiring understanding of the fear of the Lord will help us to discern what is true and what isn't. Consequently, I want to talk a little bit about what the fear of the Lord is and how it changes us. If we are going to lead with wisdom, we must let the "fear of the Lord" teach us.

Proverbs 15:33

The fear of the LORD is the instruction of wisdom; and before honour is humility.

The following three verses also talk about understanding in conjunction with the fear of the Lord. Job, Psalms, and Proverbs are poetic books. In many languages poetry is formed with rhyme, but in the Hebrew language part of what makes something poetry is a form known as *parallelism*. In what is called *synonymous parallelism*, the same or similar ideas are conveyed one after the other with different words. In these verses we see that the fear of the Lord is the beginning of wisdom and it is equated not only with understanding, but with the knowledge of the holy, and departing from evil.

Psalms 111:10

The fear of the LORD is the beginning of wisdom: a good understanding have all they that do his commandments: his praise endureth forever.

Proverbs 9:10

The fear of the LORD is the beginning of wisdom: and the knowledge of the holy is understanding.

Job 28:28

And unto man he said, Behold, the fear of the LORD, that is wisdom; and to depart from evil is understanding.

In Proverbs 1:7 another form called *antithetical parallelism* is used in which the thoughts in the second line are contrasted with those of the previous line. When we read the verses below we understand that the fear of the Lord is something that we can choose. We also see that those who do not choose the fear of the Lord are fools.

> *Proverbs 1:7*
>
> *The fear of the LORD is the beginning of knowledge: but fools despise wisdom and instruction.*

> *Proverbs 1:29*
>
> *For that they hated knowledge, and did not choose the fear of the LORD.*

The Fear of the Lord Comes by Seeing the Lord's Glory

We have read that the knowledge of the holy is understanding, and that it causes us to depart from evil. In both the Old and New Testament we read stories of those who had encounters with God. They were often terrified, typically falling to the ground. Throughout Scripture we find that when people saw the miracles that God did, it produced the fear of the Lord.

> *Exodus 14:31*
>
> *And Israel saw that great work which the LORD did upon the Egyptians: and the people feared God, and believed the LORD, and his servant Moses.*

The word "fear" usually has negative connotations so that many might think of the "fear of the Lord" as an unfortunate experience. Some may think of the fear of the Lord as being continually terrified that God is out to get them for all the things that they have done wrong. However the books of Psalms and Proverbs are loaded with wonderful promises of blessings for those who fear the Lord.

In examining the fear of the Lord in both the Old and New Testaments, we actually discover it can be the result of forgiveness and of seeing the Lord's goodness and blessing. For the believer, the fear of the Lord has nothing to do with condemnation. On the contrary, it has to do with our transformation as we experience God's nature while receiving his forgiveness and tasting his goodness. Being secure in God's love and acceptance for us is an important aspect of the fear of the Lord.

Psalms 130:4

But there is forgiveness with thee, that thou mayest be feared.

Psalms 67:6-7

Then shall the earth yield her increase; and God, even our own God, shall bless us. God shall bless us; and all the ends of the earth shall fear him.

I remember when I first experienced God's forgiveness. The joy was indescribable! God is love, and it is the presence of his pure love that makes heaven what it is! When we turn to the Lord and receive the forgiveness of sins, the Holy Spirit imparts a love to our hearts that surpasses natural understanding.

When we boldly approach the throne of grace, knowing that our sins have been forgiven, and as we come to God through Christ, we are entering heaven.(Hebrews 9 and 10 teach this.) Heaven is not just a place far away, but a spiritual reality where the love of God becomes our sustenance. As we become overwhelmed by his goodness and by the purity and holiness of his nature we are filled with a burning desire to manifest the goodness and purity of God to all we meet. This is what causes us to depart from evil.

When I enter into God's presence through Christ, I feel like I am in heaven. Sometimes I have wept rivers of tears as I have approached the Lord. There have been times when I have felt that my whole body was vibrating with the love and the goodness of God. Sometimes this has happened as I was praying and worshiping the Lord, sometimes when just thinking about a Scripture, sometimes after seeing the wonderful things that the Holy Spirit did. Each time, I felt a love in my heart for others that I could not fully comprehend, and often thought, "How is it possible to love like this?" The joy was indescribable.

When I experienced the reality of God's being, knowing him in me and me in him, I wanted to abide there all of the time. I became afraid of doing something that might misrepresent him to others. I became careful about what I did and said, and I understood that what I was beginning to experience was what the Bible was talking about when it spoke of the "fear of the Lord."

We fear the Lord when we worship him and see the beauty of his holiness. The book of Hosea actually talks about fearing God's goodness! To fear God's goodness means that the Lord and his goodness are bigger and greater than anything else in the eyes of our hearts.

Psalms 96:9
O worship the LORD in the beauty of holiness: fear before him, all the earth.

Hosea 3:5
Afterward shall the children of Israel return, and seek the LORD their God, and David their king; and shall fear the LORD and his goodness in the latter days.

Jeremiah 5:24
Neither say they in their heart, Let us now fear the Lord our God, that giveth rain, both the former and the latter, in his season: he reserveth unto us the appointed weeks of the harvest.

The book of Acts talks about the New Testament churches walking in the fear of the Lord.

Acts 9:31

Then had the churches rest throughout all Judaea and Galilee and Samaria, and were edified; and walking in the fear of the LORD, and in the comfort of the Holy Ghost, were multiplied.

To live in the fear of the Lord is to keep him as the grandest thing in our sight as we are continually approaching God through Christ and yielding our hearts to the reality we find in his presence. Scripture talks about us being transformed into God's image as we behold his glory. When we continue to turn our hearts to the Lord and to behold his glory, we are turned away from evil. We come to hate those things that are contrary to the nature of God. In fact, Proverbs defines the fear of the Lord as hating evil.

Proverbs 8:13

The fear of the LORD is to hate evil: pride, and arrogancy, and the evil way, and the froward mouth, do I hate.

Proverbs 16:6

By mercy and truth iniquity is purged: and by the fear of the LORD men depart from evil.

The Fear of the Lord Sets Us Free From the Fear of Man

In the first chapter of the book of Revelation, we read of the apostle John's encounter with the resurrected Christ in glory. John says that Christ's head was white as wool, his eyes were like fire, his feet like fine brass, and his voice like the sound of many waters. A two-edged sword was coming from his mouth, and his countenance was bright like the sun. In Revelation 1:17-18, John goes on to say:

> *And when I saw him, I fell at his feet as dead. And he laid his right hand upon me, saying unto me, Fear not; I am the first and the last; I am he that liveth, and was dead; and, behold, I am alive for evermore, Amen; and have the keys of hell and of death.*

We read this command "fear not" often in Scripture, especially when we read of encounters similar to the one that John had. We may be afraid when we encounter the Lord, but the fear of the Lord sets us free from all other fear. For the believer, the fear of the Lord is not a fearful expectation of judgment, but it is rather a love for the righteousness and purity of God's nature that causes us to hate wickedness. The same John who was terrified and fell to the ground like a dead man at Christ's feet says this in 1 John 4:17-18:

> *Herein is our love made perfect, that we may have boldness in the day of judgment: because as he is, so are we in this world. There is no fear in love; but perfect love casteth out fear: because fear hath torment. He that feareth is not made perfect in love.*

When we see God in his glory, we see love. It is a love that is powerful and overwhelming. It is such a pure and holy love that it is frightening. But as the love of God becomes that which is greatest before us, reigning in our hearts and minds, we are delivered from fear, because perfect love casts out fear.

When I have encountered the Lord, I have sometimes become very weak. There may be times when we see the Lord as He is and we are so overwhelmed that we don't know what to do with the power and the love of God that we are experiencing. Sometimes our bodies don't know how to react. We may not be able to stand, we may cry out, we may weep loudly, we may laugh or react in a number of ways that would otherwise be embarrassing. However when we are experiencing the Lord's glory we lose the fear of everything else. We care much more about what God thinks about us then what anyone else thinks. The fear of the Lord sets us free from the fear of man and from all other fears. In Proverbs 29:25 we see another use of antithetical parallelism that contrasts the fear of man with putting one's trust in the Lord.

Proverbs 29:25

The fear of man bringeth a snare: but whoso putteth his trust in the LORD shall be safe.

Psalms 27:1

A Psalm of David. The LORD is my light and my salvation; whom shall I fear? The LORD is the strength of my life; of whom shall I be afraid?

When we see God's glory and are overwhelmed by his goodness and forgiveness towards us, our awareness of God's love empowers us to stop being so afraid about what other people think and say about us. This enables us to bless those who curse us like Jesus taught us to do. It enables us to love those who mistreat us. When we are being controlled by the fear of man, we give people the power to manipulate us, and to hurt or destroy us by their words. But when we have been delivered from the fear of man by knowing the fear of the Lord, others may curse us, yet we are not subject to their curses, and they cannot manipulate us. The fear of the Lord enables us to be free, full of joy, and overflowing with the love of God even if everyone around us is against us.

Psalm 27:1-4

A Psalm of David. The LORD is my light and my salvation; whom shall I fear? The LORD is the strength of my life; of whom shall I be afraid? When the wicked, even

*mine enemies and my foes, came upon me to eat up my
flesh, they stumbled and fell. Though an host should
encamp against me, my heart shall not fear: though war
should rise against me, in this will I be confident. One
thing have I desired of the LORD, that will I seek after; that
I may dwell in the house of the LORD all the days of my
life, to behold the beauty of the LORD, and to enquire in
his temple.*

The fear of the Lord enables us to speak the truth and to obey
God in any circumstance. It enables us to keep to the course that
God has given us. Jesus told Peter that He must go up to Jerusalem,
suffer, be killed, and be resurrected. Peter rebuked him, yet Jesus
was unmoved, saying to Peter, "Get behind me Satan," telling Peter
that he was earthly minded (Matt. 16:23). If we fear man, there will
be men like Peter who will sway us from the course the Lord has
given us. When we abide in the fear of the Lord we will remain
steadfast in our purpose like Jesus did.

A leader in the body of Christ will have opposition and will
face criticism. Because of this, it is essential for such a person to
continually be abiding in the Lord's presence and in the fear of the
Lord. The fear of the Lord enables a leader to hear criticism with
humility and teach-ability. It will also enable him or her to be
unmoved in the face of unfounded criticism, accusations, and
curses, continuing to love and be secure in the Lord, not being
hardened in heart or becoming reactionary and bitterly defensive.
Walking in the fear of the Lord will keep one on a straight course
and able to bless those who curse.

A person who falls into the snare of the *fear of man* will try to
quench all criticism or disagreement, becoming unteachable by
taking these things personally. Instead, the fear of the Lord makes
us meek and teachable, and able to listen to what we need to hear
even when it comes from those who oppose and are critical.
Moreover, the fear of the Lord sets us free from being destroyed by

men's curses and accusations or being swayed by earthly-minded opinions. It delivers us from being worn down by a critical spirit.

If we are walking in the fear of man we will take disagreement personally and feel a need to defend ourselves. We will feel shame when we are corrected, and we will project shame on others when we disagree with them. The fear of man sometimes makes us apt to enter into arguments and find minor things to disagree about. For the most part, we don't need to be argumentative, yet there are many times when it is important to argue for important truths. It is at these times the fear of the Lord will give us fortitude to speak the truth in love.

As we touched on in the last chapter concerning Paul's life, we find he often argued for the gospel and persuaded people of the truth. In the same way, the fear of the Lord can enable us to disagree with people, even sharply, without projecting shame on them or pushing them away. When we fear the Lord we can argue and demolish arguments that are set up against the knowledge of God, while at the same time exuding the love of God towards those whom we are disagreeing with.

I am sharing these things not only from scriptural wisdom, but out of my personal experience. I have found that when I am beholding God's glory, walking in the fear of the Lord, I am absolutely overflowing with love and I become humble and very sincere in my speech. Often at these times I have directly contradicted what many people were saying. I have set my face like flint, refuting the lies and arguments that were keeping people from believing the gospel. Yet the fear of the Lord enabled me to do it in such a way that many changed their minds and came into an encounter with the Lord. Instead of being shamed and pushed away, they were encouraged to draw near to God.

When our greatest desire is to walk in truth and we are not personally threatened by disagreement or criticism, there is no need to threaten or intimidate those who question us. If we see nothing in which we are wrong, we answer with humility but directly, speaking the truth from our hearts with all sincerity. And on the other hand, if we are persuaded that we need to change something, we are not afraid or ashamed to admit it. It is the fear of man that would cause us to avoid questions. Jesus did not need to avoid questions by intimidating those who would question him. Even when people asked Jesus questions to trick him, he responded with heavenly wisdom.

Sometimes leaders avoid letting many people teach or share from scripture, for fear of what they will say. However, if all believers are members of the body of Christ as scripture says, it is important for all of the members to function. It must not be only leaders who are doing the work of ministry to teach and edify. I believe that rather than avoiding potential disagreements, it is healthier when we create an atmosphere where shame is not attached to correction or to being wrong. The Holy Spirit teaches us how to correct with gentleness and love.

Learning to Give Rebukes That Bring Life

There is an old man in Maryland, a friend whom I love and a leader in the body of Christ, who has modeled for me correction that brings life. He is part of a ministry near the ocean that evangelizes, giving away thousands of free meals and Bibles. This ministry also offers meetings regularly for Christian fellowship including Bible studies in the mornings and meetings at night. The man I speak of is an elder and leader at these gatherings. He is gentle and exudes the love of God, yet sometimes he is very direct. He has been an example to me in many ways.

During most of the meetings there is opportunity for anyone to come up and share something from Scripture. Because everyone in this body of Christ is encouraged to participate, believers from all over who visit that place are able to minister to the others what God has given them. This builds up those who share along with those who hear.

I have been to many different Christian gatherings in many places, but this fellowship by the beach seems to be one of the most life-filled and encouraging places of all. Thousands of people pass through there every year. It is very edifying when during the meetings anyone who has something on their heart is able to share it without fear. It brings more of a healthy dynamic than listening to just one person speak. When only one person shares, even if what they say is good, they don't have the whole picture. The Holy Spirit gives the things that we need to hear to different people. He does not give everything that we need to one member.

Once in a while however a person will stand up and say something that provokes adamant controversy, and sometimes even something that is completely at odds with the truth of the gospel. In these cases I have seen the elder whom I speak of not hesitate to rebuke as necessary. He is a man who loves the Lord deeply and exudes love for people as well, but he is not afraid of men. His example has taught me a lot. I have seen him gently correct those who were misguided in what they said, and in such a way that there was no shame. A few times he has needed to sharply rebuke a person who was full of pride and hypocrisy like Jesus rebuked the Pharisees. I once saw him directly confront a man who was cheating on his wife.

There were a few times when he seemed harsh, but the fruit that resulted was good. Each time, whether it was a sharp rebuke or a gentle correction, the authority behind it was simply the authority that comes from speaking the truth in love. It seemed that anyone there could have said the same thing with the same authority because the authority came directly from the Spirit of truth.

The example I saw there was convincing that it is much better to let the whole body of Christ function, with the need to correct and rebuke at times, than it is to avoid situations where correction is needed by providing little opportunity for people to share what the Lord has given them for the body of Christ. If we fear man it is very difficult to let go of control, but the fear of the Lord will cause us to honor God's working through each member, as well as teaching us to be able to correct and rebuke in a way that brings life.

A leader among us will have to rebuke sharply at times. The fear of the Lord enables us to speak the truth in the face of opposition, and be purely motivated by love. If we do not fear the Lord, we will not speak the truth when it needs to be spoken for fear of how men will react and for fear they will reject us. When we choose the fear of the Lord we do not need man's approval, instead, we speak out of love for people. Sincerity and a pure heart are the mark of the fear of the Lord. There is no deceit in us when we walk in this fearless love.

Proverbs 27:6

Faithful are the wounds of a friend; but the kisses of an enemy are deceitful.

Although the fear of the Lord enables us to give a sharp rebuke when needed, it also teaches us to be gentle with others. We know how much the Lord loves people, and we know that they are made in his image, so the fear of the Lord keeps us from sinning against them with our words. The fruit of the fear of man is bitter envying and strife, but the fear of the Lord teaches us the wisdom from above:

James 3:13-17

Who is a wise man and endued with knowledge among you? Let him shew out of a good conversation his works with meekness of wisdom. But if ye have bitter envying and strife in your hearts, glory not, and lie not against the truth. This wisdom descendeth not from above, but is earthly, sensual, devilish. For where envying and strife is, there is confusion and every evil work. But the wisdom that is from above is first pure, then peaceable, gentle, and easy to be entreated, full of mercy and good fruits, without partiality, and without hypocrisy.

The Fear of the Lord Gives Understanding and Discernment

Isaiah, in prophesying about Jesus, tells us that the Spirit of knowledge and of the fear of the Lord would rest on him. We read that because Jesus would have understanding that was rooted in the fear of the Lord, He would not judge according to mere appearances. We see again in the life of Jesus that which we learned in the Old Testament, that the fear of the Lord is wisdom and understanding.

> *Isaiah 11:2-3*
>
> *And the spirit of the LORD shall rest upon him, the spirit of wisdom and understanding, the spirit of counsel and might, the spirit of knowledge and of the fear of the LORD. And shall make him of quick understanding in the fear of the LORD: and he shall not judge after the sight of his eyes, neither reprove after the hearing of his ears.*

When we come to God in faith and worship him, we experience his goodness, see his holiness, and partake of his nature. The fear of the Lord gives us an understanding that comes out of intimately knowing God's nature and participating in his love and holiness. When we have this understanding we do not judge by outward appearances but we see the heart of the issue. We learn to see things as God sees them. Here are some of the words of Christ as he responded to those who criticized him for healing a man on the Sabbath:

> *John 7:23-24 (ISV)*
>
> *If a man receives circumcision on the Sabbath so that the law of Moses may not be broken, are you angry with me because I made a man perfectly well on the Sabbath? Stop*

judging by appearances, but judge with righteous judgment!

John 8:15-16 (ISV)

You are judging by human standards, but I am not judging anyone. Yet even if I should judge, my judgment would be valid, for it is not I alone who judges, but I and the one who sent me.

Are We Rooted in Fear of the Lord or Fear of Man?

It is by the fear of the Lord that men depart from evil, but where the fear of the Lord is lacking, leaders often try to keep people in line by promoting the fear of man. However, the fear of man is a snare, and we fall into a trap when we use the fear of man to manipulate people to behave the way we feel they should. People whose motivation to do the right thing is for man's approval will also do the wrong thing to keep the peace or get man's approval.

The Bible teaches a leadership model for the body of Christ that is rooted in the fear of the Lord. Where we have leadership models that are rooted in the fear of man, we fall into a snare. A manner of leadership that forbids questions or open criticism is rooted in the fear of man, as is the style of leadership that goes along with the popular consensus and seeks to be politically correct.

Teaching that conditions people to avoid calling out wayward or abusive leaders that is justified by *false* "honor" or "love" is also rooted in the fear of man. If anyone is an example to us of what honor and love looks like, it should be Jesus. Jesus did not model honor or love by tiptoeing around the truth. He called out the Pharisees for devouring widow's houses and for their pride and hypocrisy. We have sometimes seen silence concerning even sexual abuse or illegal activities in the name of "honoring" a leader. This is the fruit of counterfeit teachings about honor that are rooted in the fear of man.

There is a story in Genesis Chapter Nine in which Noah planted the first vineyard and got drunk. He lay naked in his tent, and his son Ham went and told his other brothers about it. But Shem and Japheth covered their father's nakedness. When Noah sobered up, he cursed Ham for what he had done, but blessed his other two sons. We sometimes hear that just as Shem and Japheth covered the nakedness of their father Noah, we ought to cover the nakedness of our leaders instead of being like Ham, where we talk to others about their "nakedness" or personal weaknesses. This may be a true principle, but if we depart from the fear of the Lord, we end up abusing this principle and taking it beyond the teaching of the whole of Scripture.

When we have honor that is rooted in the fear of the Lord, we will see the best in people and want to believe the best about them. We will not be searching out their faults and weaknesses or desire to expose their faults to others. Yet when a leader sins and does not repent, or stubbornly goes on in wrongdoing, then we must speak out. And when a person is teaching things that are contrary to the gospel, we must make our disagreement public for the sake of the body of Christ.

Ephesians 5:7-12

Then do not become partakers with them; for you then were darkness, but are now light in the Lord; walk as children of light. For the fruit of the Spirit is in all goodness and righteousness and truth, proving what is pleasing to the Lord. And have no fellowship with the unfruitful works of darkness, but rather even reprove them. For it is shameful even to speak of the things being done by them in secret.

A counterfeit "honor" that is rooted in the fear of man makes us afraid to give a very needed rebuke. It makes us afraid to speak out and declare the truth when we recognize a lie. When all the teaching we hear is about "honor," but we do not hear that balanced with talking about how Jesus rebuked the Pharisees and Paul rebuked Peter, what we are hearing taught is often a perversion of true honor. It is not rooted in the fear of the Lord but is really rooted in the fear of man.

Jesus did teach that when a brother sins against us we are to go to him at first privately to talk about it.[7] However the context of this is personal offense. We are also told to not accept an accusation against an elder unless it comes from two or three witnesses.[8] But we are not told that we must go to a person privately to question public teaching. If teaching does not stand up to Scripture it can be publicly challenged.

Understanding this should cause us to choose our words very carefully. Did Jesus approach the Pharisees privately at first before he rebuked them publicly? In the book of Galatians did Paul approach Peter privately, or did he rebuke him to his face in front of everyone? They both give us important examples.

The example of Jesus does not fit a counterfeit concept of honor that is rooted in the fear of man. As leaders, if we are walking in the fear of the Lord and speaking from a pure heart with sincerity, we should not be afraid of being questioned publicly. If we try to quench questions with intimidation, we are teaching the fear of man. If we welcome scrutiny of what we say, we are much more careful about what we teach!

The fear of the Lord keeps us from becoming critical faultfinders, but it also makes us bold and unafraid to speak the truth. Avoiding speaking the truth because of the fear of man is actually deceit. Sincerity from a pure heart, which is the fruit of the fear of the Lord, compels us to speak the truth in love. We should have nothing to hide.

In Second Chronicles Chapter Five we read that as the singers sang, "The Lord is good, his steadfast love endures forever,"[9] the

---

[7] Matthew 18:15

[8] 1 Timothy 5:19

[9] 2 Chronicles 5:13-14

place was filled with a cloud of God's glory so that the priests could not stand to minister. Many times when I was worshiping the Lord or even just thinking about some of the wonderful promises in Scripture, my soul was filled with the glory of God in such a way as to be physically overwhelming. I tangibly felt the goodness of God touching me, especially on my face. My heart was overwhelmed with the love of God. At times like these, when God became so big in my eyes, I knew what the fear of the Lord is.

These experiences left me changed. Because I knew by experience the nature of God, I became much more tenderhearted, and much more patient with people. This transformation made me less critical in many ways, and less reactive to criticism from others. I came to appreciate the good in people more instead of always seeing their faults. As we behold God's glory we become like him!

Yet, at the same time I became as bold as a lion! I began to lose the fear of talking to others about the Lord or declaring the gospel openly. I also found that when I heard teaching or ideas about God that were contrary to the gospel, I was able to refute them instead of being silent for fear of disagreement. But God gave me grace to speak the truth both with gentleness and sincerity and in a way that many people were able to hear. They were blessed when they did, because the word of God brought life to them and helped them to see where they were being hindered. I was learning by experience what it meant to walk in sincere love. Walking in the fear of the Lord enables us to be both as bold as lions and as gentle as lambs.

I believe that teaching about leadership in the body of Christ can be tested by these principles. Whatever would lead us into being moved by the fear of man is a trap. Whether teaching about submission, honor, or position in the body of Christ, our understanding must begin with knowing the fear of the Lord.

Chapter 4
Positions in the Church and Leadership Roles

First in the church

> 1 Corinthians 12:28
> And God hath set some in the church, first apostles, secondarily prophets, thirdly teachers, after that miracles, then gifts of healings, helps, governments, diversities of tongues.

I think that for many of us when we first read this verse, it is almost inevitable that we think of rank. This is often because of the way most of us are shaped to think by the cultures we grow up in. If someone would just open their Bible for the first time and put their finger down on this verse to read, it would seem like it is talking about rank as in an army.

However, if we are reading through the whole Bible and finally come to this verse, we do not so quickly assume that it is speaking of hierarchical rank. We have already read the gospels and known not only Jesus' personal example, but also his words to his disciples in Mark 9:33-35:

And he came to Capernaum: and being in the house he asked them, "What was it that ye disputed among yourselves by the way?" But they held their peace: for by the way they had disputed among themselves, who should be the greatest. And he sat down, and called the twelve, and saith unto them, "If any man desire to be first, the same shall be last of all, and servant of all."

We also keep Mark 10:31 in mind: *But many that are first shall be last; and the last first.*

If we have first built on Jesus teaching, we are already thinking of something very different from being first in rank. One of the reasons that we must first build our understanding on the words of Jesus is that Jesus specifically defined the meaning of words like "first" when used as pertaining to *among us.*

The word "first" can mean many things, depending on the context. In some contexts it can mean first in rank. It can also mean first in function, or first chronologically. A person who goes ahead of others goes first. If we are all brothers as Jesus said, then what does "first" mean in the context of the church? Let's take a closer look at "first" in the body of Christ.

The Body of Christ

1 Corinthians 12:12-27

For as the body is one, and hath many members, and all the members of that one body, being many, are one body: so also is Christ. For by one Spirit are we all baptized into one body, whether we be Jews or Gentiles, whether we be bond or free; and have been all made to drink into one Spirit. For the body is not one member, but many.

If the foot shall say, Because I am not the hand, I am not of the body; is it therefore not of the body? And if the ear shall say, Because I am not the eye, I am not of the body; is it therefore not of the body? If the whole body were an eye, where were the hearing? If the whole were hearing, where were the smelling? But now hath God set the members every one of them in the body, as it hath pleased him.

And if they were all one member, where were the body? But now are they many members, yet but one body. And the eye cannot say unto the hand, I have no need of thee: nor again the head to the feet, I have no need of you. Nay, much more those members of the body, which seem to be more feeble, are necessary: And those members of the body, which we think to be less honourable, upon these we bestow more abundant honour; and our uncomely parts have more abundant comeliness.

For our comely parts have no need: but God hath tempered the body together, having given more abundant honour to that part which lacked: That there should be no schism in the body; but that the members should have the same care one for another. And whether one member suffer, all the members suffer with it; or one member be honoured, all the members rejoice with it. Now ye are the body of Christ, and members in particular.

This is the context leading up to 1 Corinthians 12:28 which says God has placed apostles first in the church, then prophets, and so on. If we take this verse out of context, it is easy to assume that God gives his orders to the apostle, and the apostle passes them down to prophets, and so on in rank and file. It could also be assumed that the word of an apostle carries more weight than that of a teacher or someone in another supposedly lower position. However, the context here is a metaphor that compares believers to the member of a human body. Does the human body function by hierarchy? How do the members of the human body work together?

Each member of the body gets its signal to move directly from the brain (head). When the finger needs to move, the head does not send the message to the heart, which then imparts the vision to the lungs, which then commands the arm, so that the arm can confirm to the finger what it should do. The message from the head is received directly by the finger, and the finger moves! The finger does not need to ask the heart if it has permission to move. Rather, the head directly orchestrates the function of every member of the body in order that all the parts work perfectly together.

So then, if the human body does not have a hierarchy of command of some members over others, can any members in a human body be considered *first*? I think possibly the heart and lungs can be. Why? They are the first to work. They are first because they serve the other members by enabling them to do their jobs. The only thing that the heart has to do with the finger moving is that it supplies blood to the finger. It does not command the finger, but it *serves* it. The commands, however, come from the head. In the human body, all of the parts mutually serve each other and all are important. No member can say it does not need the others.

What we understand is that when the head sends the message to the legs to run, the muscles begin to require more blood and oxygen. Do the legs command the heart and lungs that are serving them to work harder to meet their need? No. The heart does not command the legs, nor do the legs command the heart. When the legs need fresh blood the message goes from them directly to the head, and then the head sends the message to the heart and lungs and other members of the body to do their parts as well.

What I understand in this analogy that Scripture uses is first, that every member of the body of Christ relates directly to Christ who is the head. Second, the role of those members that are first is not to command the other members but to serve them and help them to fulfill their functions. Christ himself is the head that directly orchestrates the working of each member as he sees fit, so that they all work together. Isn't this perfectly consistent with the teaching of Jesus and also of the Epistles?

Ephesians 4:11-16 (LITV)

And indeed He gave some to be apostles; and some prophets; and some evangelists; and some pastors and teachers; with a view to the perfecting of the saints for the work of the ministry, for the building up of the body of Christ, until we all may come to the unity of the faith and of the full knowledge of the Son of God, to a full-grown man, to the measure of the stature of the fullness of Christ, so that we may no longer be infants, being blown and carried about by every wind of doctrine, in the sleight of men, in craftiness to the deceit of error, but speaking the truth in love, we may grow up into Him in all things, who is the Head, the Christ, from whom all the body, having been fitted and compacted together through every assisting bond, according to the effectual working of one measure in each part, produces the growth of the body to the building up of itself in love.

In Ephesians, we again see that the role of people who have functions referred to as "first" is to equip others for the work of ministry and to build them up. The whole body also works to edify itself—with each member serving the others. We also read that Christ is the head of the body and that the growth comes from him. In other words it is Christ who directly orchestrates the function of every individual member.

There is a common teaching that a young believer needs to first serve his leader's vision until the time comes when he is released as a leader to follow his own vision. The implication is that we must start by serving another person until the time eventually comes when people we lead will be serving us.

To the contrary! Rather, the Bible teaches that the function of what some call the fivefold ministry is to equip the saints for the work of ministry and to serve them by helping them succeed in what God has called them to do. The emphasis is on the leaders serving the God-given visions and callings of the younger disciples, helping them to succeed at what God has gifted them to do. The idea that in the church you serve a leader until the time when you become a leader with others serving you, is the opposite of what Jesus taught! Jesus, as the greatest apostle in history, came not to be served but to serve.

Baby Christians start off being served, being helped, being supported. But as a believer grows he or she goes *lower* by increasingly serving more and more people and becoming a great help and support to others. Those who are greatest enable and encourage others to fulfill the callings of God on their lives. Just like the heart and lungs in a human body serve the other members, so we are to enable other believers to fulfill their functions.

Okay, if the commands come directly from the head and not from any other member of the body, than what about wise counsel? There is no doubt that it is wise to seek advice at times and to hear the counsel of elders. However, no one else in the body of Christ is to be a go-between whose approval we first must attain in order to obey God. Yes, we should listen to the advice of those who may be wiser or more mature than us. Yet we do this in order to discern if something they share with us is wisdom that is confirmed to us by the Holy Spirit—not because we need an intermediary between Christ and us. God does sometimes speak to us through what other people have to say, but even then He speaks directly to our hearts to confirm what we hear.

Many times a more mature person has shared something with me through which the Holy Spirit spoke to me. I saw that what they said was good, and the Holy Spirit illuminated their words to me, confirming in my heart the way that I should go. There have also been times when a well-meaning person spoke to me like Peter did to Jesus in Matthew 16:22 and 23. This is where Peter began to rebuke Jesus for following the Holy Spirit to Jerusalem, but Jesus turned and said to Peter, *"Get thee behind me, Satan: thou art an offence unto me: for thou savourest not the things that be of God, but those that be of men."* We should not neglect to seek wise counsel, recognizing when the Lord confirms good advice by speaking to our hearts; yet, neither should we be swayed from obeying the Lord when we hear contrary earthly-minded advice such as Peter's fearful caution to Jesus.

Apostles: The Feeble, Less Honored, Uncomely Members

Although I am not defining the specific functions of all of the different ministry gifts, but rather sharing about the nature of Christian leadership in general, I would like to talk a little about apostles. I want to do this because the Bible names them as *first* in the church. Here again are verses 22-25 of 1 Corinthians 12, speaking of the body of Christ:

> *Nay, much more those members of the body, which seem to be more feeble, are necessary: And those members of the body, which we think to be less honourable, upon these we bestow more abundant honour; and our uncomely parts have more abundant comeliness. For our comely parts have no need: but God hath tempered the body together, having given more abundant honour to that part which lacked: That there should be no schism in the body; but that the members should have the same care one for another.*

Have you ever wondered what these weaker, less impressive members of the body of Christ are? My opinion may be surprising to some people. There is a good deal of Scripture that leads me to believe that these feeble, uncomely members are in particular, the apostles. Why? Because this is how Paul describes himself as an apostle. It is also how Jesus is described in Isaiah 53. Hebrews 3:1 says that Jesus is the apostle and high priest of our profession, so I think it is safe for us to say that Jesus is the best model we have of apostleship.

Isaiah 53:2-4

For he shall grow up before him as a tender plant, and as a root out of a dry ground: he hath no form nor comeliness; and when we shall see him, there is no beauty that we should desire him. He is despised and rejected of men; a man of sorrows, and acquainted with grief: and we hid as it were our faces from him; he was despised, and we esteemed him not. Surely he hath borne our griefs, and carried our sorrows: yet we did esteem him stricken, smitten of God, and afflicted.

Paul, in 1 Corinthians, talks about the members of the body which are feeble, thought to be less honorable, and uncomely (plain-looking). This is exactly how Jesus is described in Isaiah 53. He was not esteemed or honored, and people were not impressed by his appearance. He came in weakness. Paul often related his role as an apostle to Christ's weakness and un-impressiveness. Paul spoke of the many trials and hardships that he faced as an apostle and described God's power manifesting in his weakness. We see this in both Epistles to the Corinthians, where in one instance Paul says God actually sets forth the apostles last! So apostles are first in the church because they are last, and Jesus said the last would be first!

1 Corinthians 4:8 -13

Now ye are full, now ye are rich, ye have reigned as kings without us: and I would to God ye did reign, that we also might reign with you. For I think that God hath set forth us the apostles last, as it were appointed to death: for we are made a spectacle unto the world, and to angels, and to men. We are fools for Christ's sake, but ye are wise in Christ; we are weak, but ye are strong; ye are honourable, but we are despised. Even unto this present hour we both hunger, and thirst, and are naked, and are buffeted, and have no certain dwellingplace; And labour, working with our own hands: being reviled, we bless; being persecuted, we suffer it: Being defamed, we intreat: we are made as the filth of the world, and are the offscouring of all things unto this day.

2 Corinthians 13:4

For though he was crucified through weakness, yet he liveth by the power of God. For we also are weak in him, but we shall live with him by the power of God toward you.

2 Corinthians 4:12

So then death worketh in us, but life in you.

2 Corinthians 12:9

And he said unto me, My grace is sufficient for thee: for my strength is made perfect in weakness.

1 Corinthians 2:3-4

And I was with you in weakness, and in fear, and in much trembling. And my speech and my preaching was not with enticing words of man's wisdom, but in demonstration of the Spirit and of power.

1 Corinthians 1:25-28

Because the foolishness of God is wiser than men; and the weakness of God is stronger than men. For ye see your calling, brethren, how that not many wise men after the flesh, not many mighty, not many noble, are called: But

God hath chosen the foolish things of the world to confound the wise; and God hath chosen the weak things of the world to confound the things which are mighty; And base things of the world, and things which are despised, hath God chosen, yea, and things which are not, to bring to nought things that are.

Apostles: Slaves of Christ

The word "apostle" literally means "one who is sent." It is generally understood that an apostle is an ambassador, sent to represent another. The Christian apostle is sent by God as an ambassador of Christ. The English word "missionary" comes from a Latin translation of *apostle* (missio).

Brian J. Dodd, Ph.D.,[10] writes about the role of a Christian apostle in his paper *Apostles, Slaves of Christ.*[11] He says that normally the person who would send another on his behalf would be either a slave owner or a government or military leader. Brian continues to explain that the sent one (apostle) had no choice in the matter. Since travel in the ancient world was dangerous, an apostle sent by a military or government commander was usually part of an armed entourage. The slave-apostle would not have this protection. A slave owner would often choose the most expendable and lowest slave to represent him because he could easily be killed along the way. This kind of apostle was as lowly as and might even have been the same as the slave who would wash people's feet.

Brian makes the point that this is the kind of apostle that Paul equated himself with. He writes:

---

[10] Brian J. Dodd, Doctor of New Testament Studies, Sheffield University, South Yorkshire, England, UK, has served as a pastor, church planter and seminary professor. He has led training in leadership development and evangelism in the U.S., U.K. and in countries of the former Soviet Union. He lives in Florida.

[11] Brian J. Dodd, *Apostles, Slaves of Christ.* Online: http://www.harvest-now.org/fileadmin/resources/en/friends/Apostles%E2%80%94Slaves_of_Christ.pdf

Paul's most common self-description throughout his letters is: "I am a slave who is sent by Jesus to non-Jews to communicate the good news that the Kingdom of God has come in Jesus." English readers of the Bible find it easy to overlook this important aspect of Paul's self-understanding, since the 190 different Greek terms used for slavery in the New Testament are sanitized to "servant". This is not a very appropriate translation, since in Paul's day 1/3rd of the population of the Roman empire were masters who owned slaves, 1/3rd of the people were slaves, and 1/3rd were former slaves.

He goes on to so say that these kinds of apostles were not rare but quite common, and that many would not equate apostleship with title, status or privilege. To be an apostle meant to become expendable, low status, and exposed to ridicule and insecurity in this life. Brian says that such apostles are gifts to the church and to the world, and are needed most desperately.

I think that Brian's description of slave-apostleship sounds a lot like the life of Paul and the other New Testament apostles. This understanding seems to line up very well with Paul's teaching in the New Testament. Paul, James, John, Jude, and Peter all identified themselves as slaves of Christ. And this is consistent with the teaching and example of Jesus as the greatest of all apostles. Let's look at what the Literal Translation of the Holy Bible (LITV) says:

Romans 1:1

Paul, a slave of Jesus Christ, a called apostle, separated to the gospel of God.

Galatians 1:10

For do I now persuade men or God? Or do I seek to please men? For if I yet pleased men, I would not be a slave of Christ.

Titus 1:1

Paul, a slave of God and an apostle of Jesus Christ...

James 1:1

James, a slave of God and of the Lord Jesus Christ, to the twelve tribes in the Dispersion.

2 Peter 1:1

Simon Peter, a slave and apostle of Jesus Christ, to those equally precious with us, having obtained faith in the righteousness of our God and our Savior, Jesus Christ.

Jude 1:1

Jude, a slave of Jesus Christ, and brother of James, to the ones called in God the Father, having been set apart, and having been kept to Jesus Christ.

Revelation 1:1

A Revelation of Jesus Christ, which God gave to Him to show to His slaves things which must occur quickly. And He signified by sending through His angel to His slave, John.

Mark 10:44

And whoever of you desires to become first, he shall be slave of all.

Chapter 4

Colossians 4:7
All the things about me, Tychicus the beloved brother and
faithful minister and fellow-slave in the Lord, will make
known to you.

Colossians 1:7
even as you also learned from Epaphras our beloved fellow-
slave, who is a faithful minister of Christ for you.

Philippians 2:7
But emptied Himself, taking the form of a slave, having
become in the likeness of men.

Many people will look for references to apostles as admirals or military commanders, people of great rank who run the show and are in command. However, in so doing, the concept of an apostle being the lowest of slaves is ignored and rarely mentioned. Therefore I ask you: which kind of apostle does the New Testament actually point to? Which use of the word is consistent with the teaching of Jesus about how apostles should be among us? Which kind of apostle was Jesus?

I believe that when we really understand what the role of a Christian apostle is to be, the only way that we will desire apostleship is when we have been consumed with a supernatural impartation of God's love. The examples of Jesus and of all the apostles in the New Testament show that what it means to be an apostle is to lower oneself, to become a servant to all, and to face many hardships and difficulties for the sake of our Lord and Master.

I have met several modern apostles who fit this description quite well. Earlier I wrote about Heidi Baker and a few of the many great difficulties that she faced. As I read the accounts of rapid church growth today in many parts of the world, and the persecution that often comes with it, I am led to believe that there are many more apostles in the world today than most people would believe. Nevertheless, most are unknown, unimpressive, and not highly honored. True apostles today, just like those of the first century, often have little or no support and face great hardships and discouragement because their obedience to Christ leads them into very difficult situations and environments.

Giving More Abundant Honor to the Parts That Lack It

1 Corinthians 12:22-25

Nay, much more those members of the body, which seem to be more feeble, are necessary: And those members of the body, which we think to be less honourable, upon these we bestow more abundant honour; and our uncomely parts have more abundant comeliness. For our comely parts have no need: but God hath tempered the body together, having given more abundant honour to that part which lacked: That there should be no schism in the body; but that the members should have the same care one for another.

We should give greater honor to apostles not because of their high position, but because of their low position. True apostles are often quite unimpressive, weak, and lacking in honor. They are thrust into difficult places. It is right to honor them because of their sacrifice and service.

Just as Jesus, the greatest apostle, took the lowest position, apostleship is the lowest position in the church. We should give these apostles greater honor because they lack it in the context of their work. What they are called to do is difficult, and our encouragement and support helps them. We can help apostles by our prayers, and we can share in meeting their needs.

It is because of the difficulty of serving as an apostle that the Bible talks about a right of support for apostles coming from the people they go to. When Jesus sent his disciples as apostles he told them to stay with those who received them and to eat what was set before them, for a worker is worthy of his wages. This was the "right" that Paul referred to, though he chose to not make use of it.

God's Building

Let's look at another scriptural metaphor for the church: the church as a *building*. This is found in several places in the New Testament. We see it in the Gospels when Jesus said that he was going to raise up a temple not made with hands. We also read about God's building in the Epistles, including Ephesians Chapter 2, First Corinthians Chapter 3, and First Peter Chapter 2.

Ephesians 2:20-22

And are built upon the foundation of the apostles and prophets, Jesus Christ himself being the chief corner stone; In whom all the building fitly framed together groweth unto an holy temple in the Lord: In whom ye also are builded together for an habitation of God through the Spirit.

1 Corinthians 3:9-11

For we are labourers together with God: ye are God's husbandry, ye are God's building. According to the grace of God which is given unto me, as a wise masterbuilder, I have laid the foundation, and another buildeth thereon. But let every man take heed how he buildeth thereupon. For other foundation can no man lay than that is laid, which is Jesus Christ.

1 Peter 2:5

Ye also, as lively stones, are built up a spiritual house, an holy priesthood, to offer up spiritual sacrifices, acceptable to God by Jesus Christ.

In a building, the first stones to be laid are on the bottom, and they support the others. In this respect, the Bible teaches us that those who are first in the church, apostles and prophets, are foundational, and that Jesus Christ himself is the chief cornerstone. So in this scriptural metaphor, those who are first in the church are not over others, but *under* them. Isn't this amazing! Just as the members that are first in a body serve the others, so the stones that are first in a building are those that support the others. Again we see that those who would be great among us must become the servants of all.

Hierarchy is like a pyramid, with one stone on the top, supported by all of the others. A leader who has a hierarchical mindset expects others to serve and support his vision. Yet to the contrary, in the body of Christ, leaders are on the bottom supporting all of the others. This is perfectly in line with the function of leadership in the body of Christ as serving and supporting other disciples, helping them towards success with their God-given dreams and goals.

This is not to say that young disciples should not support and serve leaders as well, but this is not the emphasis in Scripture. Sometimes we hear of contemporary teaching that puts an emphasis on young believers laying down their dreams in order to support a leader's vision, however I think this is both unscriptural and unhealthy. Certainly all of us in the body of Christ are to serve and lay down our lives for each other, but if emphasis is on the young disciples supporting leaders, we have things backwards. The scriptural emphasis is on leaders supporting and serving the others. The greatest among us are those who are the greatest servants.

This brings up an important point. When a leader is a guy on top then it is easy to have one leader. On the other hand, when leaders are on the bottom, as in God's building, things are different. It is easy to have one stone at the top of a pyramid, but it is not possible to build a building on one stone, unless it is a really huge stone! We are told that the church is built on the foundation of the *apostles and prophets.* We do not read that a church is built on the foundation of *an* apostle or prophet, as in singular. Instead we see the New Testament generally talks about leaders among us in plurality as in Ephesians Chapter Four where there are several ministry functions mentioned. A variety of leaders should support us and lay a foundation that we can build on, and of course Christ himself *must* be the chief cornerstone!

My Pastor

It is interesting to think that in the culture in which I grew up, and probably you too, the "pastor" seems to be the most essential part of the church. However, in the English Bible the word "pastor" only appears one time: in Ephesians chapter four. I was conscious of this even when I was a child because I always heard people talking a lot about "the pastor" and yet I read very little about pastors in the New Testament. I thought that this was strange. Even though "pastor" was one of the most-mentioned words I heard when in Christian company, it was found only once in the Bible. It was not even included with the apostles and prophets as a foundational ministry in Ephesians 2:20.

Later I learned that the English word "pastor" has the same meaning as "shepherd." Nevertheless, Ephesians 4 is the only place in the Bible where this word shepherd seems to be describing a function in the church. Since "pastor" is another translation of the Greek word "poimen" which means "shepherd," it is misleading for those who do not realize it is the same thing.

In reading the New Testament in Russian, Spanish, or Portuguese, I see that the word is not translated two different ways like it is in many English Bibles. In Spanish and Portuguese it is simply "pastor," or plural "pastores." I counted at least eleven times in the New Testament that this word was used in the singular in the context of referring to Jesus as our "Pastor." This means the word is used at least eleven times in the singular referring to Jesus, and only *one time* in the plural in the context of leaders given to equip us for the work of ministry.

I know this may sound unconventional, but when someone asks me the question, "Who is your pastor?" I feel that it is clear the scripturally accurate answer is, "My Pastor is Jesus." This recalls for me once again Jesus' teaching in Matthew 23:

Matthew 23:10

Neither be ye called masters: for one is your Master, even Christ.

Strong's concordance tells me that the word translated as "master" means "guide," and figuratively "teacher." [12] It is the Lord who I rely on to guide me as my pastor. As Psalm 23:1 says, "The Lord is my Shepherd, I shall not want." The Spanish version says that: "The Lord is my Pastor, I shall not want."

Yes, I do thank God for placing pastors in the church, and I am grateful for those who have functioned as pastors to me. Yet as the New Testament does, I only use the singular possessive "my Pastor" in referring to the Lord, while any other person I refer to as "a pastor."

Why is this important to me? It's significant because many different people have contributed to my life and helped me to learn and grow in my faith. All of them were imperfect human vessels.

---

[12] Word G2519 in *Strong's Hebrew and Greek Dictionaries,* used in Matthew 23:8

Many of them had teaching in one area that led me to truth and blessed me, yet also taught other things that were the traditions of men and which confused and hindered me. The Lord worked through one person in helping me in one area, but He then had to use another person to correct me concerning something that the previous one led me astray in.

The Lord has used the teachings, examples, and encouragement of numerous people with different gifts in helping me to mature. No one of these people could have come close to single-handedly fulfilling the role of being "my pastor." I pay attention to the examples of those who have gone before me, but no single one of them is my example or my guide. Rather, Jesus is my Example and my Guide.

Singularity of leadership is easy in a hierarchy, but when leaders are the stones at the bottom of a building, a plurality of leadership is necessary to support that building. As leaders, it is important for us to encourage people to relate to and receive from a variety of ministers.

I do not want to be anyone's pastor, but I do have a heart to pastor people and lead them toward Christ. I know that I have things to impart to people and teach them, but I only have part of the picture, and if my heart's desire is to see the church grow up in all things into Christ, than I will want people to receive from many others; not just from me. I want the young disciple to relate to Jesus as his or her pastor, while at the same time honoring and receiving from the treasure that God has put in the jar of clay that I am.

Sometimes young believers are really blessed by one leader, talking about and listening to that person all the time. It may be that what that person has to offer is what the young believer needs at the time. But I think that as we mature we begin to recognize how much we have to learn from a greater variety of leaders, as well as to realize that leaders we relate to are jars of clay and it is not possible to build true faith on any one of them. We stop putting them on pedestals when we see that Christ is our chief cornerstone.

As I read the New Testament I find reason to believe that the word "elders" is synonymous with "pastors." If that is so then the Bible does talk about pastors in several places, although it only uses the term as the noun "pastors" once in referring to men other than Christ. The reason I see these as equivalent is because Peter exhorted elders to pastor God's flock.

1 Peter 5:1-4

The elders which are among you I exhort, who am also an elder, and a witness of the sufferings of Christ, and also a partaker of the glory that shall be revealed: Feed the flock of God which is among you, taking the oversight thereof, not by constraint, but willingly; not for filthy lucre, but of a ready mind; Neither as being lords over God's heritage, but being ensamples to the flock. And when the chief Shepherd shall appear, ye shall receive a crown of glory that fadeth not away.

This implies that elders are pastors (shepherds), because they are commanded to feed the flock. Again it stands out to me that "elders" is plural, and also that elders are not commanded to feed their flocks, but to feed the *flock of God*. What this tells me is that if I am a pastor, I shepherd people, but they are not my sheep. Christ is the Chief Shepherd, and I would not dare to call any whom He has entrusted to me "my sheep."

Deaconing

The English word "deacon" came from the Greek "diakonos." The verb "to deacon" is "diakoneo." A quick search of where these Greek words are used shows that in the KJV they are by far most often translated as servant or minister (diakonos), and "to serve" or "to minister" (diakoneo). I found thirty-seven uses of the verb "diakoneo" in the New Testament. Of them, twenty-three times it was translated as some form of the verb "to minister" and ten times as some form of "serve." Two times it is translated as "use the office of a deacon."

> *1 Timothy 3:10*
>
> *And let these also first be proved; then let them <u>use the office of a deacon</u>, being found blameless.*

> *1 Timothy 3:13*
>
> *For they that have <u>used the office of a deacon</u> well purchase to themselves a good degree, and great boldness in the faith which is in Christ Jesus.*

The English word *deacon* is not really a translation, but a transliteration of this Greek word that signifies service: "diakonos." Why in the world would "diakoneo" be translated to mean some form of service nearly everywhere else, but in these two 1 Timothy verses be transliterated as "deacon" with the words "use the office of" arbitrarily added? The word "office" is not found in the original Greek at all, but is added to the translation. It is clear that this was once again a consequence of translators trying to make Scripture fit into their human traditions.

I also searched for every place that the noun "diakonos" is used in the New Testament. I found thirty uses of this word, and of them, "diakonos" was translated as "minister" or "ministers" twenty times. It was translated as "servant" or "servants" seven times, and "deacons" *three times.* Why the transliteration in these few places instead of the translation that is given in most other instances of the word in the New Testament? The transliterations are found in contexts where using a transliteration, along with adding the word "office" twice, make it seem to support human traditions and hierarchical ways of thinking.

As a child growing up in church, what I heard led me to believe that deaconship was a position in the church that was lower than that of an elder. And of course the elder was under a pastor, who would certainly be under an apostle! Because of this context, I thought, "Who wants to be a deacon? I want to be an apostle!" Yet the Greek use of the word shows me that Paul and the apostles were deacons! Studying Scripture has convinced me that it is perfectly true to say that apostles, as well as prophets, pastors, and others in ministry, are all deacons! In other words, they are all servants.

When we take an honest look at Scripture it is baffling to think about how *deaconship* came to be categorized as a position in a hierarchy. However, it seems that many with a Western mindset like to categorize everything instead of realizing that the New Testament writers simply used different words, sometimes synonymous, to describe service in the body of Christ.

Phillipians 1:1

Paul and Timotheus, the servants of Jesus Christ, to all the saints in Christ Jesus which are at Philippi, with the bishops and deacons.

The word "deacons" here is again diakonos. A person with a Western mindset who is trying to categorize everything and is reading their tradition back into Scripture, looks at this Scripture and assumes that Paul was an apostle, Timothy was a pastor, and bishops and deacons are other positions or ranks. However, Paul referred to himself six times in the New Testament as a "diakonos," while referring to Timothy as a "diakonos" twice! Even Jesus is called a "diakonos." Paul, Timothy, and Jesus were all deacons! In the following Scriptures, the words translated from "diakonos" are underlined.

Chapter 4

1 Thesselonians 3:2
And sent Timotheus, our brother, and <u>minister</u> of God, and our fellow labourer in the gospel of Christ, to establish you, and to comfort you concerning your faith.

Ephesians 3:7
Whereof I was made a <u>minister</u>, according to the gift of the grace of God given unto me by the effectual working of his power.

1 Corinthians 3:5
Who then is Paul, and who is Apollos, but <u>ministers</u> by whom ye believed, even as the Lord gave to every man?

2 Corinthians 6:4-10
But in all things approving ourselves as the <u>ministers</u> of God, in much patience, in afflictions, in necessities, in distresses, In stripes, in imprisonments, in tumults, in labours, in watchings, in fasting. By pureness, by knowledge, by longsuffering, by kindness, by the Holy Ghost, by love unfeigned, By the word of truth, by the power of God, by the armour of righteousness on the right hand and on the left, By honour and dishonour, by evil report and good report: as deceivers, and yet true; As unknown, and yet well known; as dying, and, behold, we live; as chastened, and not killed; As sorrowful, yet alway rejoicing; as poor, yet making many rich; as having nothing, and yet possessing all things.

Romans 15:8
Now I say that Jesus Christ was a <u>minister</u> of the circumcision for the truth of God, to confirm the promises made unto the fathers.

Yet aren't Apostles first in the church? Yes, and Jesus taught that the first would be last as a "diakonos" to all! Therefore if anyone is a deacon, it appears this person must especially be an apostle as Jesus and Paul were!

Mark 9:35

And he sat down, and called the twelve, and saith unto them, If any man desire to be first, the same shall be last of all, and <u>servant</u> of all.

Matthew 20:26

But it shall not be so among you: but whosoever will be great among you, let him be your <u>minister</u>.

Although Jesus was "deaconed" (served) by others, he came into the world not to be "deaconed," but to be a deacon (servant) to others. In the following Scriptures, the underlined words are translated from the verb "diakoneo."

Matthew 20:28

Even as the Son of man came not to be <u>ministered</u> unto, but to <u>minister</u>, and to give his life a ransom for many.

Matthew 27:55

And many women were there beholding afar off, which followed Jesus from Galilee, <u>ministering</u> unto him.

Luke 22:26-27

But ye shall not be so: but he that is greatest among you, let him be as the younger; and he that is chief, as he that doth serve. For whether is greater, he that sitteth at meat, or he

84

that <u>serveth</u>? is not he that sitteth at meat? but I am among you as he that <u>serveth</u>.

In the book of Acts we read of the apostles appointing deacons to serve tables, and on a surface level when reading this in English it may appear that this position which seven men were appointed to was deaconship. However, the apostles simply said that they would appoint men to serve (diakoneo) tables so that the apostles could devote themselves to prayer and to the ministry (diakonia) of the word. Serving tables and serving with the word of God are just different kinds of deaconship. We see again that the apostles were deacons as well.

Acts 6:1-4

And in those days, when the number of the disciples was multiplied, there arose a murmuring of the Grecians against the Hebrews, because their widows were neglected in the daily <u>ministration</u>. Then the twelve called the multitude of the disciples unto them, and said, It is not reason that we should leave the word of God, and <u>serve</u> tables. Wherefore, brethren, look ye out among you seven men of honest report, full of the Holy Ghost and wisdom, whom we may appoint over this business. But we will give ourselves continually to prayer, and to the <u>ministry</u> of the word.

Bishopping

The word "bishop," which in Greek is the noun "episkopos," is used five times in the New Testament. Of those five times, one time is referring to Jesus (who was an apostle). Being an "episkopos" is also used in a way that is to be equated with eldership just as the apostle Peter called himself an elder. In spite of this basic application of the word, it seems that the traditions of men have construed it, like the others, to suggest a level in a hierarchy. However, in the context of

Scripture all of these words are so often clearly used in interchangeable ways. In the following verse the translation of the verb "episkopeo" is underlined. This is where we see the apostle Peter, who is an elder, exhorting fellow elders to "bishop" God's flock.

1 Peter 5:1-3

The elders which are among you I exhort, who am also an elder, and a witness of the sufferings of Christ, and also a partaker of the glory that shall be revealed: Feed the flock of God which is among you, <u>taking the oversight</u> thereof, not by constraint, but willingly; not for filthy lucre, but of a ready mind; Neither as being lords over God's heritage, but being ensamples to the flock.

In the book of Titus as well, the words "elder" and "bishop" are used interchangeably. And in Acts Chapter Twenty, Paul calls elders "episkopos" (bishops).

Titus 1:5-7

For this cause left I thee in Crete, that thou shouldest set in order the things that are wanting, and ordain elders in every city, as I had appointed thee: If any be blameless, the husband of one wife, having faithful children not accused of riot or unruly. For a <u>bishop</u> must be blameless...

Acts 20:17-18, 28

And from Miletus he sent to Ephesus, and called the elders of the church. And when they were come to him, he said unto them... Take heed therefore unto yourselves, and to all the flock, over which the Holy Ghost hath made you <u>overseers</u>.

Notice here again, that the contexts are plural. In 1 Peter, Peter is commanding elders to bishop God's flock; while in Titus, Paul is talking about appointing elders. In Acts, Paul is exhorting the elders of Ephesus. Nowhere in the Bible do we see a singular person who is THE bishop of a church, or THE pastor of a church.

As they did with the word "diakoneo", the KJV translators arbitrarily added the word "office" in the following passage, in such a way as to make it fit into their paradigm. This addition of the word "office" makes it seem that the function or position of a "bishop" is different than that of an elder or a deacon (servant).

> *1 Timothy 3:1,5*
>
> *This is a true saying, If a man desire the office of a bishop, he desireth a good work...(For if a man know not how to rule(proistemi) his own house, how shall he take care of the church of God?)*

In the continuation of this passage Paul uses the word "diakonos" (servant) in verse 8 and 12, and "diakoneo" (to serve) in verses 10 and 13. Verses 10 and 13 are where the translators also arbitrarily added the word "office" before the transliteration "deacon". Because of the interchangeability of all these terms in scripture, I find it most reasonable to understand the whole passage in 1 Timothy 3:1-13 as simply referring to the same people, elders. Elders are appointed to serve (diakoneo), watch over (episkopeo), and care for (vs. 5) God's people.

The word "episkopos" means an "overseer."[13] Although its uses in the New Testament may not give us enough context for a full understanding of the nature of that oversight, some contexts of

---

[13] HELPS Word-studies www.HelpsBible.com 1985 *episkopos* - properly, an *overseer,* a man called by God to literally "keep an eye *on*" His flock (the Church, the body of Christ), i.e. to provide personalized (first hand) care and protection (note the *epi,* "*on*").

the use of a verb form of the word and the way it was sometimes translated give us more insight into the role of an "episkopos" or bishop. The following examples suggest that the nature of the "watching over" that an overseer does, is taking care of people, especially those who are sick or weak.

In Matthew 25, in the parable of the sheep and goats, Jesus is teaching us that whatever we do for the least of his brethren we do for him. In this instance, the word "episkeptomai" is used to describe how *we serve* others, and by implication how we serve Christ. He is not suggesting we are to be in some hierarchical role of bishopping!

Matthew 25:36, 39-40

Naked, and ye clothed me: I was sick, and ye <u>visited</u> me: I was in prison, and ye came unto me... Or when saw we thee sick, or in prison, and <u>came unto</u> thee? And the King shall answer and say unto them, Verily I say unto you, Inasmuch as ye have done it unto one of the least of these my brethren, ye have done it unto me.

What, then, is the nature of the "overseeing" that bishops are responsible for? Where we find in the KJV the word "episkeptomai" is translated as "visited," several other Bible versions translate it as "looked after" or "took care of."[14] In the above Matthew 25 passage, try substituting "looked after," "watched over," or "cared for" where the words are underlined in verses 36 and 39. It makes sense, doesn't it? In the Epistle of James, who is the sick believer commanded to call to render care by praying and anointing with oil? The elders are.[15] They *look after* or *care for(bishop)* the sick one. Again, we see the interchangeability of the terms "elder" and "bishop. Here are more uses of the word "episkeptomai."

---

[14] For example "looked after" in NIV and YLT, and "took care of in GNB
[15] James 5:14

Acts 15:36
And some days after Paul said unto Barnabas, Let us go again and <u>visit</u> our brethren in every city where we have preached the word of the Lord, and see how they do.

James 1:27
Pure religion and undefiled before God and the Father is this, <u>To visit</u> the fatherless and widows in their affliction, and to keep himself unspotted from the world.

These verses where the verb "episkeptomai" is used confirm the insight we get from Matthew 25 about what the role of an "episkopos" or bishop is. This is also confirmed by 1 Timothy 3:5, which describes the role of a bishop as to *"take care of the church of God"*. Once again our study leads us to yet another word describing "service to" and "care for" others, as opposed to ruling over them! What also amazes me is that Matthew 25 makes it so clear that when I "bishop" the least of these, I "bishop" Jesus! Additionally, the word "diakoneo" (serve, minister, deacon) is also used in Matthew 25.

Matthew 25:44-45
Then shall they also answer him, saying, Lord, when saw we thee an hungered, or athirst, or a stranger, or naked, or sick, or in prison, and did not <u>minister</u> unto thee? Then shall he answer them, saying, Verily I say unto you, Inasmuch as ye did it not to one of the least of these, ye did it not to me.

Matthew 25 teaches me that it is possible for me to be a *bishop* and a *deacon* unto Jesus. If this is so, then being a "bishop" and "watching over people" cannot very well be a position of authority over people can it! Rather, it is again a position of service. Being a bishop describes a role of serving others by caring for them.

We "bishop" and "deacon" Jesus by serving others, just as at times in his life on earth Jesus needed to be cared for by those around him. We see this by the use of "diakoneo" in describing how certain woman served Jesus and looked after him by providing for some of his needs.

I have realized that when I was in Russia with friends visiting orphans and old shut-in grandmothers, we were "bishopping" them. I was filling the biblical role of a bishop. Yet I certainly did not have the sense of being *over* those seventy and eighty year old ladies in any way! Rather it was my privilege to serve and encourage them, as well as to lay hands on them and see them healed. It is also scriptural to say that as I "bishopped" them, it was my privilege to be "bishopping" Jesus!

Leaders Alongside Each Other and Below Younger Disciples

A closer look at words like "apostle," "pastor," "bishop" and "deacon," and especially the interchangeability of them with each other and with words like "elder," totally destroys the notion that they are positions on different levels in a hierarchy of authority over each other and over others. An honest study keeps leading us again and again back to Jesus' teaching that the first and greatest among us is to be the servant of all.

Nevertheless, and as inconsistent as it seems in light of the written word we have just examined, soon after the New Testament Gospels and Epistles were written, people began categorizing and using these biblical words in a way much different than the simplicity of service the writers depict. How did this come about? It transpired partly because people who considered themselves knowledgeable did not view these texts in the light of the foundational teachings of Jesus himself. Because Jesus' teachings were too counter-culture for them, they couldn't fully comprehend them and fathom that Jesus actually meant what He said. Even Jesus' original disciples, after personally spending three and a half years with him, were quick to start jostling for position, so it is not surprising that other disciples would do the same soon after the New Testament was written!

We see clearly that the rest of the New Testament does not contradict Jesus' emphatic teaching that we are all brothers. In the body of Christ, the members who are first are those who serve the others. In God's building, those living stones that are first are closer to the bottom, supporting others. Leaders are found alongside other leaders and below the younger disciples. We never see them positioned over others in the teaching of the New Testament.

It is clear that some have tried to fit the teaching of the New Testament into a hierarchical paradigm, and this is evident in many Bible versions where several different words are translated to the same word, or the same word is translated different ways in different places. However, as we study which Greek words are used, we see that a better understanding of the language throws many wrenches into the idea that leadership in the body of Christ has hierarchical structure. We find that many common interpretations of certain Scriptures don't pan out and are really a result of us reading pre-existing cultural mindsets back into Scripture to make it say things that it doesn't actually say.

Chapter 5
Letting Go

Building Christ's Kingdom Must Be Our Priority

Mark 9:33-40

And he came to Capernaum: and being in the house he asked them, What was it that ye disputed among yourselves by the way? But they held their peace: for by the way they had disputed among themselves, who should be the greatest. And he sat down, and called the twelve, and saith unto them, If any man desire to be first, the same shall be last of all, and servant of all.

And he took a child, and set him in the midst of them: and when he had taken him in his arms, he said unto them, Whosoever shall receive one of such children in my name, receiveth me: and whosoever shall receive me, receiveth not me, but him that sent me. And John answered him, saying, Master, we saw one casting out devils in thy name, and he followeth not us: and we forbade him, because he followeth not us. But Jesus said, Forbid him not: for there is no man which shall do a miracle in my name, that can lightly speak evil of me. For he that is not against us is on our part.

Why did Jesus' disciples forbid a man who was not of their group from casting out devils in Jesus' name? I suspect that the reason was jealousy. They had just been arguing about who would be the greatest among them. They were proud to have been the ones whom Jesus chose and sent to cast out demons and heal the sick, and they wanted to keep their positions exclusive to their in-crowd.

This man who was casting out demons but not part of their party was a threat to their special status. They did not consider him as being *qualified* as they were. Maybe they even believed he needed to be trained by them before he could be appointed to cast out demons. More likely the real issue was that the disciples were competing for position.

Jesus made it clear however that there was to be no competition. He said, "He that is not against us is on our part." He that is not against us is for us. Jesus forbade his disciples from stopping anyone who would do a mighty work in his name. The priorities of Christ's disciples were wrong. Instead of laying down their selfish ambitions for the sake of Christ's kingdom, they were caught up in the politics of self-preservation and of seeking the most honorable positions. They were seeking to build kingdoms for themselves.

Jesus' disciples were still modeling their roles after the way the princes of the gentiles governed, but Jesus made it clear that it was not to be that way among them. In the governments of this world people fight to protect their positions, sometimes even creating needs that they can meet so that their offices can continue. But leadership in the body of Christ should never be a position that needs to be preserved. Rather, leaders in the body of Christ are to work themselves out of a job as soon as possible.

Ephesians 4:11-13

And he gave some, apostles; and some, prophets; and some, evangelists; and some, pastors and teachers; For the perfecting of the saints, for the work of the ministry, for the edifying of the body of Christ: Till we all come in the unity of the faith, and of the knowledge of the Son of God, unto a perfect man, unto the measure of the stature of the fulness of Christ.

Notice that God gave apostles, prophets, evangelists, pastors and teachers for the building up of the body of Christ until we all come to the unity of the faith and of the knowledge of the Son of God. When the body of Christ comes to the full measure of the stature of Christ, these are no longer needed. This implies that the more the body of Christ matures, the less the fivefold ministries are needed. If we are seeking the things that are God's priorities, our goal must be for the body of Christ to come to such maturity that we are needed less and less in the roles where we served before.

How do we do this? How did Jesus model it? Let's look at his example.

The Example of Christ

Sometimes we read the Bible many times and pass over something it says again and again without really thinking about it. Then one day we are reading and it hits us, or maybe somebody points out what that Scripture is saying and we realize that we just never thought about it before.

And so it was for me when I read chapters fourteen, fifteen and sixteen of the Gospel of John. This is one of my favorite passages in Scripture. Jesus is telling his disciples that he is about to leave, and he tells them about the soon coming of the great Comforter, the Holy Spirit, who he will send to them.

John 14:25-26

These things have I spoken unto you, being yet present with you. But the Comforter, which is the Holy Ghost, whom the Father will send in my name, he shall teach you all things, and bring all things to your remembrance, whatsoever I have said unto you.

Jesus had been present with his disciples for just three and a half years. Now he was about to ascend to the Father and was assuring them that the Holy Spirit would remind them of everything that he himself had taught them. Then Jesus told his disciples that it was actually good for them that he was leaving!

John 16:6-7 (YLT)

But because these things I have said to you, the sorrow hath filled your heart. But I tell you the truth; it is better for you that I go away, for if I may not go away, the Comforter will not come unto you, and if I go on, I will send Him unto you.

I had read this so many times without really considering how amazing this statement was! The disciples had Christ himself in the flesh with them, walking with them daily, teaching and guiding them. Yet now after just three and a half years, it was *better* for them that Jesus go! The disciples were uncomfortable with the idea of Jesus leaving. They not only had not accepted it, they simply didn't understand why it was necessary for God's purposes to be fulfilled or even what these purposes were. As one wise brother, Steve Hill, has often pointed out: Jesus wanted them to learn to follow the internal guidance of the Holy Spirit rather than continuing to rely on his external guidance and presence with them.[16] This was necessary for their maturity.

There comes a time when a mother bird may have to push her little chicks out of the nest. This is what Jesus was doing. If a baby bird never leaves the nest it will die. Yes, growing up may be

---

[16]http://www.harvest-now.org/nachrichten-der-ernte/n/?L=3%27%22&tx_ttnews[tt_news]=269&tx_ttnews[year]=2008&tx_ttnew s[month]=12&tx_ttnews[day]=03&cHash=f2e0af8acb037c4963bd7d578648f193

uncomfortable. The disciples didn't want Jesus to leave, but it would not have been healthy for them to never learn to stand on their own feet. After three and a half years, Jesus was pushing his disciples out of the nest so that they could learn to fly!

Before He left, Jesus was already weaning the disciples from dependence on him and teaching them to eat solid food. There is a time when a baby needs milk, but it is not healthy if that time never ends. The growing child must learn to feed himself. For some children, this time of learning to eat solid food may be uncomfortable, but it is necessary.

When we look at Jesus' example, we realize that the people whom we disciple should be growing less and less dependent on us, and more and more dependent on the Holy Spirit. We learn that our role is not to draw people to ourselves, but to teach them to listen to and rely on the Holy Spirit themselves. When we are building up others in the body of Christ, there will soon come a time when we need to push those babies out of the nest!

The Mongolian Church Planting Movement

It was Brian Hogan[17] whom I first heard point out the implications of Jesus' statement in John 16 for present-day leaders in the body of Christ. Brian and his family moved to Mongolia in the early 1990's as part of a Youth With A Mission (YWAM) church-planting team. Just a short time before, there had been no known indigenous believers in Mongolia, but in 1991 a friend of the Hogan's had lead

---

[17] Brian Hogan serves full time with Church Planting Coaches, a global ministry of Youth With A Mission. He serves YWAM on the Frontier Mission Leadership Team. Brian has participated in, led, and started organic expressions of Jesus' Body in the USA, Malta, and Mongolia both inside and outside the traditional wineskin. He coaches those involved in these movements on five continents, especially focusing on where the church isn't. Brian is the author of two books, "There's a Sheep in My Bathtub: Birth of a Mongolian Church Planting Movement," and "An A to Z of Near Death Adventures."

a short-term mission team and they had publicly baptized thirty-six new Mongol believers.

The church grew quickly in the few years after Brian, with his wife and another couple, moved to Mongolia. Then, three and a half years after their team had arrived, the baton of leadership was passed on to the Mongolian leaders and Brian and his family left the same day. The church rapidly multiplied and many new fellowships were planted. By 1998 there were more than 10,000 Mongol believers, and now Mongolia sends more missionaries per believer than any other country in the world! [18]

My introduction to Brian was at a missions conference and church-planting seminar in Lancaster, Pennsylvania several years ago. Brian shared his experience and also talked a lot about stripping "church" of all the things we have added to it from our culture, and getting down to the biblical basics of what church really is. He shared an in-depth scriptural study of church and leadership.

Brian kept speaking about how important it was to get the new believers participating as soon as possible. Their church plant in Mongolia had grown quickly, and they had to give serious responsibilities to believers who were sometimes only a few weeks old in the Lord. Many other missionaries who had been around much longer were very uncomfortable with this. It seemed to them that this young YWAM team was making some foolish decisions. Yet Brian had observed in Scripture how quickly Jesus began to

---

[18] http://www.examiner.com/article/mongolia-from-2-to-50-000-christians-20-years "Conservative estimates state that the number of believers grew from just two in 1990 to over 50,000 believers in 2005. Mongolia has changed from a mission field to being a powerful mission force— sending out more missionaries per believer than any other nation on Earth"

train his disciples by having them imitate him. Even though the disciples were still quite immature, Jesus got them in the game quickly and corrected them as they went.

The new Mongolian believers met in houses for discipleship and fellowship and also had large "Celebration" meetings. As new believers became involved in ministry and even in leadership very quickly, there was not an undue amount of responsibility on any one person. Because everyone was participating in the new assemblies, ministry was a light load rather than a heavy burden.

At the church-planting seminar, Brian told us that everyone in Mongolia loved big, western style "Celebration" meetings. However, as they began to have these large congregational church services every week, the church would stop growing! People would stop taking responsibility for their own faith and expect a few leaders to do everything. Because of this, they stopped the big meetings and the church started growing again.

Yet when people expressed how they missed the big exciting gatherings, they started them up again. When these meetings became regular weekly events, the people soon neglected meeting in their houses where they ministered to each other and took responsibility for their own faith. Once again, the church stopped growing until they stopped the big meetings, after which the church would start to grow again.

Finally the decision was made to limit the big fun meeting to once or twice a month. It had become clear that if it was held more frequently, people tended to neglect actually functioning as members of the body of Christ. Instead they became mere spectators. Brian explained that having the big meeting more often than once a month seriously hindered growth and the vitality of members serving and building one another up. In the New Testament the churches gathered in larger citywide form when there was sufficient reason to do so, such as a visit from the Apostle Paul. The calendar was not the deciding factor.

When the mission team was finally planning to leave after only three and a half years, many people protested, especially other missionaries who were in the country. They said things like, "How can you leave now? There's still sin in the church! There are still many problems that need to be dealt with." Some expected the young church to quickly die without the continuing guidance of the American missionaries.

Brian was concerned and sought the Lord about whether or not what they were planning to do was wise. God showed Brian that Jesus, after three and a half years, told his disciples that it was better for them that He leave. Why? Because they now needed to trust the Holy Spirit to fill the role that Jesus promised them the Holy Spirit would fulfill. This is what Jesus told them was *better!* Even though Jesus' disciples still had things to learn and still didn't get a lot of what Jesus had spoken about during their time together, Jesus trusted the Holy Spirit to remind them of all that He had said to them.

Brian also understood that the apostle Paul acted in the same way as Jesus did, usually remaining with a new church for a relatively short time before he moved on. When the Holy Spirit directed Brian's attention to Ephesians Chapter Twenty where Paul is saying goodbye to the Ephesians, he realized that leaving Mongolia was exactly what the Lord was leading them to do.

Paul's Example

Acts 20:25-32

And now, behold, I know that ye all, among whom I have gone preaching the kingdom of God, shall see my face no more. Wherefore I take you to record this day, that I am pure from the blood of all men. For I have not shunned to declare unto you all the counsel of God. Take heed therefore unto yourselves, and to all the flock, over the which the Holy Ghost hath made you overseers, to feed the church of God, which he hath purchased with his own blood. For I know this, that after my departing shall grievous wolves enter in among you, not sparing the flock.

Also of your own selves shall men arise, speaking perverse things, to draw away disciples after them. Therefore watch, and remember, that by the space of three years I ceased not to warn every one night and day with tears. And now, brethren, I commend you to God, and to the word of his grace, which is able to build you up, and to give you an inheritance among all them which are sanctified.

Paul was going on in obedience to God, leaving the Ephesian disciples after just three years from the time when he began to proclaim the gospel to them. He knew that they would never see his face again. He knew serious problems were about to arise, and he warned them of this. Yet Paul left the Ephesians just as Jesus had done with the twelve, likewise commending them to the word of God's grace and to the Holy Spirit!

Paul did not want the churches to continue to be dependent on him! There was a time when the young believers needed to be taught, but there soon came a time when they should be teachers. How long was it until that time when the new believers were expected to be teachers? The examples of both Jesus and Paul show us just a few years.

Hebrews 5:12

For when for the time ye ought to be teachers, ye have need that one teach you again which be the first principles of the oracles of God; and are become such as have need of milk, and not of strong meat.

In 1 Corinthians, Paul talks about this immaturity and carnality as indicated by the Corinthians' continuing to look to himself and to Apollos instead of to the Lord himself. Paul was working to wean the Corinthian believers off of dependence on him, and into a mature relationship with the Holy Spirit.

1 Corinthians 3:1-6

And I, brethren, could not speak unto you as unto spiritual, but as unto carnal, even as unto babes in Christ. I have fed you with milk, and not with meat: for hitherto ye were not able to bear it, neither yet now are ye able. For ye are yet carnal: for whereas there is among you envying, and strife, and divisions, are ye not carnal, and walk as men? For while one saith, I am of Paul; and another, I am of Apollos; are ye not carnal? Who then is Paul, and who is Apollos, but ministers by whom ye believed, even as the Lord gave to every man? I have planted, Apollos watered; but God gave the increase.

What is Hindering Growth?

Brian is now a church-planting coach, who works with YWAM in training and advising church planters all around the world. These men and woman work in many different people groups and cultural contexts. I recently heard an interview in which Brian was talking about church planting.[19] He described being in back to back meetings in a hall, each time full of church planting teams, with people firing questions at him from all sides. They were from different regions and the problems and dynamics were varied and often very different. But Brian kept finding himself giving the same two answers to all of the questions.

He started to feel funny continuing to say just the same two things to them. He was embarrassed about sounding so repetitive, but he kept feeling that the Holy Spirit was giving him the same answers, showing him that it was one or both of these things that were keeping the church from growing and reproducing. Finally, in

---

[19] https://www.youtube.com/watch?v=MHboMIEPxAo

the second week of these gatherings as Brian was spending time in his room, he called out to God, asking him to give him something else to say. Brian says that God answered, "No, those are the answers. Those two things are the obstacles that are blocking the DNA of my church from what I created it to do: to grow and to reproduce"

Brian went on to explain that the first of the obstacles those church-planting teams faced was that their churches were way too complex. They needed to radically simplify. The second was that they didn't trust the Holy Spirit to be what Jesus had promised his Spirit would be in the life of the believer.

Brian states that distrust of the ministry of the Holy Spirit in people's lives is built into our institutional Christianity. We don't release people, and certainly not new believers, into significant ministry because they might screw up. On the other hand, pastors complain about the five people in the church who do everything with the rest doing nothing. But the people have been trained into this passivity so much that they are puzzled and resistant when asked to do something.

Brian says that this distrust of the role of the Holy Spirit is the reason why people are dumbfounded by his team's experience in Mongolia wherein the church grew so fast that brand new believers quickly ended up leading house churches. Yet because everyone was involved and responsibility was shared, leadership was not a huge heavy weight, but instead the burden was easy and light just as Jesus promised!

In closing the discussion, Brian challenged listeners to take the time to go through Scripture and list the ministries of the Holy Spirit they observed, and then to ask themselves, "In what ways have we been doing these very things that the Holy Spirit can do perfectly well on his own?"

Growth by Multiplication, Not Simply Addition.

The cells in a human body grow by multiplication, not just by simple addition. A cell splits and becomes two, then four, eight, and so on. When I read stories of places around the world where the church is growing rapidly, the growth so often follows this pattern. There are church splits, but not splits caused by division and disagreement, but by growth! It is growth coming not from adding more and more people to one group focused upon a few leaders, but from releasing new leaders very quickly. When I hear the counsel of Brian Hogan in conjunction with other wise people who have been involved in world missions for decades, I see the importance and effectiveness of this strategy confirmed.

This is what Jesus modeled. He discipled a few, and taught them to disciple others. Soon, he was pushing them out of the nest, telling them that it was time for him to go. Neither did Paul focus on establishing a big centralized group, but rather on discipling those who would disciple others. After only a few years at most, he left new fellowships and went on to the next place. Of course there was still relationship through letters, messengers, and visits, but there was a specific letting go and entrusting of the new believers to the Holy Spirit.

We are members of the body of Christ, in which the Holy Spirit has given each of us a function and grace to bless the rest of the body. We are commanded to minister to each other with the grace that God has given us.

Colossians 3:16

Let the word of Christ dwell in you richly in all wisdom; teaching and admonishing one another in psalms and hymns and spiritual songs, singing with grace in your hearts to the Lord.

Chapter 5

1 Peter 4:10

As every man hath received the gift, even so minister the same one to another, as good stewards of the manifold grace of God.

Now, when the life of God is flowing and each member is overflowing with the grace that God has given, we may have a problem. There is not time enough for people to share what God has given each one to minister. This is important to recognize: when we are seeking growth by addition, the more our numbers grow, the more limited the functioning of the body of Christ becomes. Because of time constraints, ministry becomes more and more limited to a few people so that we lose the health and vitality that flows when every member of the body is functioning. Because of this, many who were part of movement and full of life at the beginning, subside and become muted and ineffectual as the numbers grow.

We have often seen movements that began in revival lose life and power as the numbers increased because they didn't release people. When they were small there was place for every member to minister. But because there was a paradigm in which leaders feared people leaving (instead of sending them out), and in which leaders sought to add numbers to create a large group centered on a program, participation became more difficult the more the numbers grew. This, in turn, stifled the growth of the movement. It's happened again and again in the Western context. There are flames of revival and something starts, but it rarely lasts long because leaders don't know how to release people or create a context in which every member of the body can function. This kind of paradigm is highly focused around just a few people. Where growth occurs, it is typically believers from other venues attracted by a better program rather than by increase in new believers.

Instead of hindering and restraining the role that individual believers can play as a group grows, it is time to let go so the cell divides. Like Brian shared, big meetings are fun, but when they replace the smaller gatherings where every member of the body of Christ is functioning and ministering, the big meetings become a hindrance. Instead of drawing many people to be dependent upon a small group of leaders, we need to learn to disciple them and then let go, sometimes even pushing them out of the nest.

This doesn't mean we can't have large gatherings once in a while, especially since we really enjoy them; but as we grow, the participation of every member should increase, not decrease. Having every member effectual is very hard to do when a big meeting becomes the main thing that people think of when they think of "church." When we only have a large gathering, there is only opportunity for a very few people to function in certain roles.

When many believers begin to mature and function in God's grace as pastors, teachers, apostles, ect., there needs to be a context for them to do so. When we let go and grow by division, as cells do, we create a context in the smaller groups in which people can minister and grow in the grace of God that is on their lives. It is important that we do so for the sake of the health of the body of Christ, and in order that we receive all of the blessing that God has to give us through the various members of his body.

Politics and Dependency

If we have modeled leadership in the body of Christ after the political systems of the world as Jesus warned us not to do, we have set up the precise environment that keeps people dependent on us. When leadership is about position and privilege, and not example and service, we end up needing people to need us. If people don't need us we lose our positions.

The apostle Paul was concerned about the disciples still being on milk when they ought to be teachers. Yet, contrary to Paul's concern, all too often leaders today are perfectly happy to have people who have been believers for decades still in dependence on them. Why? Sometimes it is because people depending on us both create and substantiate the role we try to fill. Then when other believers attempt to fulfill their roles in the body of Christ, it becomes a threat to our position that we are trying to protect.

At other times, we keep believers in dependence on us for far too long because we don't trust the Holy Spirit to do his job. We become fearful that if we don't keep holding people's hands they will fall. When we become overprotective and continue to treat growing disciples like babies, we hinder their development and coming to maturity in Christ.

Sadly, we find that all too often it is easier to let the pastor and a few others do the work than for people to obey Christ's call themselves. This was what was happening in Mongolia. Every time they held to a big meeting on a weekly schedule led by just a few leaders, the people stopped going to the small gatherings where they functioned by the Spirit according to the grace God had given them. It seems it is always more comfortable to be a baby and let others take care of us than to be put in situations where we are challenged and consequently grow.

Consequences of Exaggerating the Role of One Leader

In the last chapter we talked about the huge emphasis that our culture places on "the pastor" as contrasted to the Bible. I noted that the noun "pastor" is found only once in the entire New Testament, and in the plural, referring to human leaders other than Jesus; whereas the other instances of the Greek word (poimen) are translated as "shepherd." Because of this discrepancy, people don't immediately realize they are translated from the same Greek word.

We talked about pastoring being a valid and important function for leaders among us, but one that is often greatly overemphasized. We also examined the scriptural emphasis on Jesus as filling the primary role of being our pastor (shepherd), with the role of other men in pastoring being limited and always subordinate to Jesus' role.

In Latino cultures the role of a pastor is often even more emphasized than in the United States. This is especially true when people continue to have Roman Catholic mindsets. The pastor or "man of God" may often take the role of a Catholic saint and become the mediator between the believer and God. Many people who once prayed to Mary and asked Mary to forgive their sins are now trying to approach God through an Evangelical pastor while still lacking a relationship with the Lord that stands on its own. These people look to the pastor almost as to God. If their pastor were to fail, likewise their faith would fall apart because they built their faith on that pastor and not on Christ.

As a result of this misplaced trust, to such people the voice of their pastor is very nearly the voice of God. They not only feel quite inadequate to pray themselves for another person, but especially unfit to pray for their pastor when he needs help! Not so long ago here in Brazil, I was talking to an Evangelical woman who was completely stunned and in awe because her pastor asked her to pray for him. She said, "Who am I? I am nothing to pray for a pastor!" Those who look to another human in such a way never come to maturity or learn to hear God's voice for themselves. Their belief systems are formed not by "The Bible says..." but "My pastor says...." Consequently, when a pastor's sin or even weaknesses are exposed, people's faith falls apart. Their faith was never resting on Christ in the first place, but instead upon their pastor.

In South America, I am constantly seeing how deeply these mindsets are engrained in so many people. While in North America I find this dependency can be just as real, it seems much less endemic. From this observation, I have come to see that it is very important for us to be intentional about helping young disciples in the process of maturity by teaching them to develop their own relationship with God. We also need to encourage them to learn from a variety of different elders in the body of Christ without idolizing any one of them.

I think it is important to help people to not become comfortable with letting "the pastor" or a few people try to do that which is the responsibility of the whole body of Christ. As we learn to trust the Holy Spirit to do what he said he would do, we learn to let people try, fail, and try again. A baby does not learn to walk without falling many times. He does not learn to eat solid food without a mess. Understanding this, we need not be too alarmed by messes, but rather recognize them as part of the learning process.

Sometimes parents try to do everything for a child for fear that the child will fail or get hurt. Some do this to the point where it continues into college. Absurdly, there are parents who go to their grown kid's job interviews with them, wash their laundry, and manage their finances. The result of such behavior? It is that the learning capability of these young people is inhibited, their growth is stunted, and they do not develop the confidence needed for challenges they will face in the future.

When the role of "pastor" encroaches on the healthy functioning God intended for the whole body of Christ, the maturation and spiritual health of believers is hindered. Not only this, but such a dysfunctional relationship also hurts the one expected to play such a proprietary role in the life of the believer. It is often said that the most difficult job there is, is to be a pastor. Yet I do not often hear the question asked, "Does God intend it to be that way?" Following is a collection of statistics provided by *The Fuller Institute, George Barna, and Pastoral Care Inc.*:

July 21, 2009
Why Pastors Leave the Ministry
by Fuller Institute, George Barna and Pastoral Care Inc.

90% of the pastors report working between 55 to 75 hours per week.

80% believe pastoral ministry has negatively affected their families. Many pastor's children do not attend church now because of what the church has done to their parents.

33% state that being in the ministry is an outright hazard to their family.

75% report significant stress-related crisis at least once in their ministry.

90% feel they are inadequately trained to cope with the ministry demands.

50% feel unable to meet the demands of the job.

70% say they have a lower self-image now than when they first started.

70% do not have someone they consider a close friend.

40% report serious conflict with a parishioner at least once a month.

33% confess having involved in inappropriate sexual behavior with someone in the church .

50% have considered leaving the ministry in the last months.

50% of the ministers starting out will not last 5 years.

1 out of every 10 ministers will actually retire as a minister in some form.

94% of clergy families feel the pressures of the pastor's ministry.

66% of church members expect a minister and family to live at a higher moral standard than themselves.

The profession of "Pastor" is near the bottom of a survey of the most-respected professions, just above "car salesman."

Many denominations report an "empty pulpit crisis." They cannot find ministers willing to fill positions.

#1 reason pastors leave the ministry: Church people are not willing to go the same direction and goal of the pastor. Pastors believe God wants them to go in one direction but the people are not willing to follow or change. [20]

I think that we need to ask ourselves if the Bible ever really put's any single person in such a role as pastoring has become. The above statistics are quite a contrast to Brian Hogan's comments about leadership being not a heavy burden at all but light and easy. Why? Because in their Mongolia church plants they were acting as the *priesthood of all believers* where everyone was involved.

Remember that even Jesus intimately "pastored" only a dozen disciples and a few close friends besides that. I believe there are far more people among us in the body of Christ to whom God has given a pastoring role than those we call pastors. It appears likely that pastoring was intended to be a less intensive responsibility given to many more people than we have concluded it to be. It seems that we need to change our expectations for pastors. We need more people functioning as pastors to smaller groups, as opposed to a few people who pastor in name only to many more people than they can handle.

The last part of the above survey grabbed my attention. The number one reason that pastors left the ministry was that the church people were not willing to go the same direction as they were. This shows us a problem. These pastors were trying to head the church instead of helping believers to grow up in all things into Christ the head. These pastors were expecting the people to support their vision (signifying their desire to be served), as opposed to equipping people to do what God had called *them* to do. That is not

---

[20] http://www.pastoralcareinc.com/statistics

what God intended pastoring to be about. So the biggest underlying reason that pastors left ministry was that they had wrong expectations about what ministry was to be.

A few years ago I attended a *Fathers and Sons in the Kingdom* conference here in Brazil. There was a young pastor who was extremely burdened and who looked very stressed and riddled with anxiety. When I asked him how I could pray for him, he told me about the church he served in his city, imploring me, "How can I be a father to all these people?" The feeling of an enormous burden of responsibility was weighing very heavily upon him. He was in tears because of the pressure he felt.

I prayed for this pastor, and I reminded him that Jesus told us to call no man our father, for we have one Father who is in heaven. Yes, Paul talked a little bit about being like a father to young believers, but that affectionate, fatherly concern is a secondary role, for God himself is our Father. Explaining this, I said to that pastor, "Don't let anyone look to you in a way in which they should only be looking to God." I went on to remind him of Jesus' words in Matthew 11:30, "For my yoke is easy and my burden is light."

As I encouraged this brother, I saw him relax as God's peace fell on him and a heavy weight lifted off of his shoulders. He had been burdened with a sense of false responsibility and with the cultural expectations of the people to be almost like God to them. An overemphasis on a leader's role in "fathering" believers added to this burden until he was almost crushed.

When we consider fathering and pastoring, it is important for us to know that the Lord himself is the one who primarily fills these roles in the lives of young disciples. As Brian Hogan advised us with the wisdom God has given him, let's trust the Holy Spirit to do what he said he would do! Yes we have responsibilities, and we do play a part in pastoring and fathering as co-laborers with God, yet scripturally it is clear that God himself is our Father, and Christ himself is our Pastor! And so, as the Holy Spirit always points to Christ, we should always be pointing first to God as our Father and to Christ as our Pastor.

Chapter 6
Authority, Commands, and Submission

The Authority of the Truth

We have talked about the importance of building our understanding on the teaching of Christ, and how his teaching put all of his disciples on the same level as brothers and fellow students, leaving no room for hierarchy. We have seen how the Epistles in the New Testament are consistent with Jesus' teaching, even though this is not always as clearly seen in the English translations as it is in the original language. We have talked about the fear of the Lord as the beginning of wisdom. We have examined the servant nature of leadership among Christ's followers, and have seen that the greatest among us do not take the highest position, but the lowest.

So now we have the question: *If there is no hierarchy in the body of Christ, then what about order?* Is there no authority to command anything? If there is authority, where is that authority derived from if not from a position over others? Let's start by asking where Jesus' authority was derived from? Jesus was asked this very question.

Luke 20:1-8

And it came to pass, that on one of those days, as he taught the people in the temple, and preached the gospel, the chief priests and the scribes came upon him with the elders, And spake unto him, saying, Tell us, by what authority doest thou these things? Or who is he that gave thee this authority?

And he answered and said unto them, I will also ask you one thing; and answer me: The baptism of John, was it from heaven, or of men? And they reasoned with themselves, saying, If we shall say, From heaven; he will say, Why then believed ye him not? But and if we say, Of men; all the people will stone us: for they be persuaded that John was a prophet. And they answered, that they could not tell whence it was. And Jesus said unto them, Neither tell I you by what authority I do these things.

It seems the chief priests, scribes, and elders asked Jesus by what authority he did what he did because they didn't like what he was doing and teaching. Or maybe it was because they were jealous. Did you notice that instead of answering them, Jesus replied with a question they could not answer? If the priests said that John's baptism was from heaven, they would have to acknowledge that John had testified of Christ. But they could not say that John's baptism was from men because they would be stoned by the people, who had been persuaded that what John said was true.

In short, Jesus was appealing to the authority of the truth which the Holy Spirit testified about directly to men's hearts. We often hear today the same question that Jesus was asked, although the question "Who gave you this authority" is usually phrased as "Who are you submitted to?" or "Who is your covering?" Those who questioned Jesus were really trying to avoid facing the truth because, as Jesus said, they cared about the testimony of man rather than that of God. In the Gospel of John we read a lot more about how Jesus' authority and the validity of his ministry were questioned, and we see how he responded.

John 5:30-34

I can of mine own self do nothing: as I hear, I judge: and my judgment is just; because I seek not mine own will, but the will of the Father which hath sent me. If I bear witness of myself, my witness is not true. There is another that beareth witness of me; and I know that the witness which he witnesseth of me is true. Ye sent unto John, and he bare witness unto the truth. But I receive not testimony from man: but these things I say, that ye might be saved.

We see through much of the book of John that Jesus repeatedly appealed to the authority of his heavenly Father and of truth itself when the validity of what he said and did was questioned. When the chief priests, scribes, and elders asked Jesus by what authority he was acting, they were asking for a testimony from man. Jesus, however, said he didn't receive the testimony of man. Jesus' authority came directly from the heavenly Father. The apostle Paul said something similar in the Epistle to the Galatians.

Galatians 1:10-12

For do I now persuade men, or God? or do I seek to please men? For if I yet pleased men, I should not be the servant of Christ. But I certify you, brethren, that the gospel which was preached of me is not after man. For I neither received it of man, neither was I taught it, but by the revelation of Jesus Christ.

The religious leaders of Jesus day cared about the approval of men. They sought honor from one another, but did not seek the honor coming only from God. A few verses later in John Chapter

Five, Jesus specifically says he does not receive honor from men. He again appeals to the authority of truth and of the heavenly Father.

John 5:41-47

I receive not honour from men. But I know you, that ye have not the love of God in you. I am come in my Father's name, and ye receive me not: if another shall come in his own name, him ye will receive. How can ye believe, which receive honour one of another, and seek not the honour that cometh from God only? Do not think that I will accuse you to the Father: there is one that accuseth you, even Moses, in whom ye trust. For had ye believed Moses, ye would have believed me: for he wrote of me. But if ye believe not his writings, how shall ye believe my words?

We see the same thing later in the Gospel of John. Jesus spoke with authority because what he said was true, and all who loved truth knew that what Jesus was saying came from God. Jesus said that his heavenly Father testified on his behalf.

John 7:14-18

Now about the midst of the feast Jesus went up into the temple, and taught. And the Jews marvelled, saying, How knoweth this man letters, having never learned? Jesus answered them, and said, My doctrine is not mine, but his that sent me. If any man will do his will, he shall know of the doctrine, whether it be of God, or whether I speak of myself. He that speaketh of himself seeketh his own glory: but he that seeketh his glory that sent him, the same is true, and no unrighteousness is in him.

John 8:12-19

Then spake Jesus again unto them, saying, I am the light of the world: he that followeth me shall not walk in darkness, but shall have the light of life. The Pharisees therefore said unto him, Thou bearest record of thyself; thy record is not true. Jesus answered and said unto them, Though I bear record of myself, yet my record is true: for I know whence I came, and whither I go; but ye cannot tell whence I come, and whither I go. Ye judge after the flesh; I judge no man. And yet if I judge, my judgment is true: for I am not alone, but I and the Father that sent me. It is also written in your law, that the testimony of two men is true. I am one that bear witness of myself, and the Father that sent me beareth witness of me. Then said they unto him, Where is thy Father? Jesus answered, Ye neither know me, nor my Father: if ye had known me, ye should have known my Father also.

We often hear the same questions today as the chief priests, scribes, and elders asked Jesus. In the same way, many appeal to the approval of man as a basis for authority while avoiding truth. Why are we concerned about who sent a minister or gave him authority to minister, rather than considering if what he preaches is backed by truth?

It is not uncommon to receive people and what they say because of who sent them, even if what they say is false. The person who sent them often matters more to us than the content of the message. If we truly want to speak with authority, it must be based on the authority of the truth, and not on the approval of men and our sense of their worth or popularity.

We often hear the teaching that if we are to walk in authority, we must be under the authority of other leaders in the church. For instance, based on the following passage, it is taught that the centurion walked in authority because he was under authority.

Matthew 8:7-9

And Jesus saith unto him, I will come and heal him. The centurion answered and said, Lord, I am not worthy that thou shouldest come under my roof: but speak the word only, and my servant shall be healed. For I am a man under authority, having soldiers under me: and I say to this man, Go, and he goeth; and to another, Come, and he cometh; and to my servant, Do this, and he doeth it.

The principle that one must be under authority to walk in authority may be true. In contexts such as that of civil government, the authority that we are under is usually that of other humans in a hierarchy of authority. However, in the body of Christ each one of us is directly under the authority of God, just as Jesus and Paul were. When we read that Jesus forbade his disciples from exercising authority over each other, we must understand that God did not intend for there to be a hierarchy of authority between any member of his body and Christ the head.

Christ should be the example for every one of us, and we should take note that people were astonished at the authority with which he taught. This is the same authority in which we are to follow Jesus, an authority that people recognized was distinctly different from the teaching of the scribes.

Matthew 7:28-29

And it came to pass, when Jesus had ended these sayings, the people were astonished at his doctrine: For he taught them as one having authority, and not as the scribes.

What was the difference between Jesus and the scribes? Remember that Jesus said he did not accept human testimony, while on the other hand the scribes sought honor from men. Jesus knew that the Father testified to what he said—that everything he said was true; while by contrast, the scribes sought the testimony of men.

Today we often see people seeking the testimony of men as the scribes did. People often try to validate their ministry by saying, "I am under apostle John So-and-So." Like the scribes whose teaching showed a lack of authority, these people try to find their validation in the testimony of men. When I go to minister somewhere, the questions are common, "Who are you under?" or "Who are you submitted to?" Why do we ask people whom they are under instead of testing whether or not what they have to say is true?

I have heard some today say we need to build a platform for ourselves by submission. I would agree if they meant we gain influence by serving others. Unfortunately, however, they are usually implying that a person who wants to be known and listened to in the body of Christ must gain his platform by coming under another person who is a well-known leader. I disagree. I believe this is a perverse and unbiblical understanding of submission that is rooted in the fear of man.

I maintain that the truth itself should be our platform. Those in Christian history who have great positive influence on us today established it not by seeking the approval of the most popular religious leaders of their day, but by speaking truth. How did Martin Luther gain such great influence? Didn't he gain great influence because he dared to say the truth that most feared to speak? And why did they fear to speak? Because they feared men instead of fearing God!

In the Third Epistle of John, we see a contrast between two men. One man, Diotrephes, loved to have preeminence. He loved to be first. He sought the approval of men. On the other hand, Demetrius was a man whom the truth itself testified about.

3 John 1:9 (YLT)

I did write to the assembly, but he who is loving the first place among them—Diotrephes—doth not receive us; because of this, if I may come, I will cause him to remember his works that he doth, with evil words prating against us; and not content with these, neither doth he himself receive the brethren, and those intending he doth forbid, and out of the assembly he doth cast. Beloved, be not thou following that which is evil, but that which is good; he who is doing good, of God he is, and he who is doing evil hath not seen God; to Demetrius testimony hath been given by all, and by the truth itself, and we also—we do testify, and ye have known that our testimony is true.

Is not the testimony of the truth the most important thing? Isn't having the testimony of the truth what should really matter, whether or not a person has the testimony and approval of men? Jesus had the testimony of John the Baptist concerning him, and he referred to that for the sake of his listeners. Yet he clarified that he did not accept human testimony, and that what really mattered was the testimony of the Father about him.

In contrast to what Jesus exemplified, too often today harmful teaching or abusive practices seem of little concern as long as a minister is "submitted to" the right person. When this happens, it demonstrates we fear man rather than God. When we fear man, we are not walking in truth or in wisdom, which begins with the fear of the Lord.

Jesus delegated to his disciples the authority to preach the gospel and to pass on his teaching to all people and nations. The authority to speak truth belongs to each one of us, and no one has the authority to stop another from speaking truth. In the body of Christ, although none of us have been given authority over other individuals, all of us have been given the authority to speak the truth in love.

Administrative Authority

Somebody may object, *"If no one is in charge, then how can we get anything done? Authority based on truth won't work if we are trying to do something and everyone wants to do it a different way.*

120

Someone needs to be in charge." This has validity. We do see administrative authority given to certain individuals in the New Testament for specific activity. However, this authority is over a task or project and not over the church. Men may be heads of Christian organizations to have administrative authority in those organizations concerning how things are done, but in the church itself, none but Christ is the head.

Acts 6:2-6

Then the twelve called the multitude of the disciples unto them, and said, It is not reason that we should leave the word of God, and serve tables. Wherefore, brethren, look ye out among you seven men of honest report, full of the Holy Ghost and wisdom, whom we may appoint over this business. But we will give ourselves continually to prayer, and to the ministry of the word. And the saying pleased the whole multitude: and they chose Stephen, a man full of faith and of the Holy Ghost, and Philip, and Prochorus, and Nicanor, and Timon, and Parmenas, and Nicolas a proselyte of Antioch: Whom they set before the apostles: and when they had prayed, they laid their hands on them.

In this case, there was a need for organization. Organization is often needed to help us to accomplish certain things more effectively. The disciples chose seven men from among themselves and appointed them over the task of managing the distribution of food. When we work together to accomplish something, it can be helpful to appoint a person over that task. However, these men were not appointed with authority over other people. Their authority was over the task they were appointed to manage.

Some people think that to make such distinctions is just arguing over semantics. However, the distinction between being appointed over a task and appointed over people is an extremely important distinction that we must make. Words have great implications. In the body of Christ a person who is set over the lives of other individuals is put in the place of Christ the head. It's important to see that this is different than managing a task. The context for the use of administrative authority is limited.

When I helped in Christian camps for youth, I obeyed the director of the camp concerning what we were doing when I was there. When I was working with those people I followed their plan. They had been appointed with authority over something that we wanted to accomplish together. I was glad that we had them to organize and manage things because it helped all of us. In the church itself, however, I am not commanded to obey a person because they are a pastor, prophet, or apostle. In the body of Christ, and in the context of how I live my life as a believer, God is the one who I am commanded to obey. Christ is my head.

I believe that Christian organizations with the purpose of accomplishing goals such as helping the poor are certainly helpful. We have no reason to be against such organizations, but we cannot rightly think of these institutions as *the church*. They may be within the church, but not all of the church is within them. It is very possible to not be a part of any such organization, yet to belong to Christ and be spiritually healthy, functioning as a member of the body of Christ and relating to other believers in a healthy way.

Joining an organization does not join anyone to the body of Christ. The Holy Spirit joins us to the body of Christ when we are born again. To teach otherwise would be to teach a counterfeit gospel. If we do not understand this we will speak of different organizations as though there are different bodies of believers. If there are different bodies it implies that there are different heads. It seems clear people don't see the problem with this when they ask, "What body do you belong to?" My answer? "The body of Christ."

Ephesians 4:3-6

Endeavouring to keep the unity of the Spirit in the bond of peace. There is one body, and one Spirit, even as ye are called in one hope of your calling; One Lord, one faith, one baptism, One God and Father of all, who is above all, and through all, and in you all.

To clarify what the role of administration is in the body of Christ, we should look at how the teaching of the New Testament speaks of the gift of "governments" among us. In the following passage the word translated "governments" is the Greek word "kubernesis" which means *pilotage* or *directorship*.[21] The Weymouth New Testament (WNT) translates it as "powers of organization." It is enlightening when we consider that this gift is a different gift than apostleship and other positions in the church. In what has become a common way of thinking, being a pastor or apostle is equated with being a governor over people. However pastoring, apostleship, and "governments" are different functions.

1 Corinthians 12:27-28

Now ye are the body of Christ, and members in particular. And God hath set some in the church, first apostles, secondarily prophets, thirdly teachers, after that miracles, then gifts of healings, helps, governments, diversities of tongues.

In First Corinthians we see that of those set in the church, "governments" are in the seventh place—not the first—with only "diversities of tongues" after it. Even the gift of helps is placed before the gift of governments! In this regard, it seems strange that apostleship and governments are so readily equated with each other, when Scripture in fact says that God placed apostles "first" (as servants of all) and governments seventh.

In the passage where Jesus told us to call no man on earth our teacher, for we have one master who is Christ, the Greek word

---

[21] Word G2941 in *Strong's Hebrew and Greek Dictionaries*

translated as "master" means "guide." [22] It seems to me that we could just as well say that we are to call no man our "pilot." Seeking an understanding that is consistent with the whole of Scripture leads me to believe that this gift of "governments" is not at all referring to the government of people, but is referring to those who serve with their administrative ability over tasks that we want to work together on. On the other hand, the government of God's people is on Christ's shoulder—Christ the head who governs all of the members of the body.

Isaiah 9:6-7

For unto us a child is born, unto us a son is given: and the government shall be upon his shoulder: and his name shall be called Wonderful, Counsellor, The mighty God, The everlasting Father, The Prince of Peace. Of the increase of his government and peace there shall be no end.

The Book of Hebrews, quoting Jeremiah, also talks about how the Lord governs his people in the New Covenant. Note the distinction between the new covenant and the old. In the old covenant with the nation of Israel, there were human governors who commanded the people to obey the Lord. The first covenant however was not faultless, so God established a better covenant, with better promises. God himself would govern his people, writing his laws on their hearts.

Hebrews 8:6-11

But now hath he obtained a more excellent ministry, by how much also he is the mediator of a better covenant, which was established upon better promises. For if that first covenant had been faultless, then should no place have

---

[22] Word G2519 in *Strong's Hebrew and Greek Dictionaries*, used in Matthew 23:8

been sought for the second. For finding fault with them, he saith, Behold, the days come, saith the Lord, when I will make a new covenant with the house of Israel and with the house of Judah: Not according to the covenant that I made with their fathers in the day when I took them by the hand to lead them out of the land of Egypt; because they continued not in my covenant, and I regarded them not, saith the Lord. For this is the covenant that I will make with the house of Israel after those days, saith the Lord; I will put my laws into their mind, and write them in their hearts: and I will be to them a God, and they shall be to me a people: And they shall not teach every man his neighbour, and every man his brother, saying, Know the Lord: for all shall know me, from the least to the greatest.

We are shown that things are different in the new covenant than they were in the old covenant. The roles of leaders are different, and some of the leaders in the Old Testament nk swere types and shadows of Christ. Also, the government of Israel in the Old Testament was a national government. All of us today are already under some kind of national government that is separate from the church.

We will sometimes hear teaching emphasizing many old covenant examples as models for leadership in the body of Christ, but that does not take into account what has changed now that we are under a new covenant. Sometimes much of the New Testament's teaching is overlooked, while the focus is put on Old Testament models in order to avoid the offense of Jesus' teaching. Consequently the words of Jesus himself are extremely underemphasized or ignored when considering what the roles of leaders are. Instead, I believe that we should first emphasize Jesus' teaching instead of talking about how things worked under a lesser covenant that has passed away.

In view of all of this, I believe that God himself governs every believer, while he also places in the church people with gifts of "governments." I believe that these gifts of "governments" are not in reference to government over people but to administrative abilities given to people whom we may set over tasks. The seven men in the Book of Acts who the disciples appointed over the distribution of food are good examples of "governments." And as we see in this example, even those who administer to accomplish a task serve those for whom the task meets needs.

Commands

In presenting my understanding of what the Scriptures teach about the role of leaders among Christ's followers, I want to address questions that typically come up. I know that the truth brings life, and I love the truth. I do not want what I present to others to seemingly be based on an opinion I have hastily come to without having tested what I believe so I'm assured of it. As I share about the way I see something I want to be honest if there are issues I still have questions about.

I do not want to be in a place where I am only talking about certain Scriptures while ignoring others. That is why in the word studies I have done I have examined every use of these words in the New Testament in order to not avoid some while talking about others. My effort is to truly come to a right understanding of what I am talking about so as to not corrupt the word of God.

> *2 Corinthians 2:17*
>
> *For we are not as many, which corrupt the word of God: but as of sincerity, but as of God, in the sight of God speak we in Christ.*

I have greatly desired to understand the role of leadership among Christ's disciples because I love the body of Christ and I know that the truth always builds us up and brings life. I want to understand the truth that will be of benefit to all of us. I have thought much about the subject I am writing about, asked many questions, searched the Scriptures, and talked with others who were more experienced than I so as to hear what they had to say.

I remember one man I met named Dan who believed differently than I had been taught on a topic I had some confusion about. Although I had not known him long, it was clear this man was full of the Holy Spirit and of the love of God like few people I had ever met. He was real and I saw no insincerity in him. I began to drill him with questions about the topic, not because I disagreed with Dan or was stuck on my own opinion, unwilling to hear anyone else, but because I actually wanted to believe what he believed! I knew that if I was going to believe it, I needed to be fully convinced that what he was saying was true, and I had questions that needed to be answered. Questioning him helped me to come to a better understanding. In the same way, I want to answer questions that may arise about leadership in the body of Christ when others search out the things I'm talking about to see if they are true.

Some might ask, "If leaders in the body of Christ are not over anyone else, then why do we see Paul commanding others in the New Testament? Why did Paul expect the churches to obey his commands?" I have considered such questions as well. In so doing, I have looked at the whole of Scripture to seek to understand what it is consistently teaches. My aim is to resolve those things that on a surface level may seem to be contradictions between the teaching of Jesus and of the apostles. I sincerely believe there are no verses I need to hide from because they don't support my conclusions. I would like to answer the questions of those who might see what appear to be contradictory verses about commands where it seems Jesus is saying one thing but Paul another.

In a previous chapter we examined the different language often used in the New Testament when talking about leaders among us that is contrasted to secular authorities. I noted that in Hebrews 13:17 we are literally told to "be persuaded by" our Christian leaders, which was translated in English as "obey." In contrast, the commands for children to obey parents and for slaves to obey masters use a more authoritarian word, the word "hupakouo." I noted there is no command for believers to obey their leaders using the word "hupakouo," rather we are commanded to "be persuaded by" (peitho) our leaders. In saying this I was speaking of a broad-sweeping, general command to obey what leaders say. However I did find just two uses of "hupakouo" which might seem to imply that disciples were expected to obey Paul.

2 Thessalonians 3:14

And if any man <u>obey</u> not our word by this epistle, note that man, and have no company with him, that he may be ashamed.

Phillipians 2:12

Wherefore, my beloved, as ye have always <u>obeyed</u>, not as in my presence only, but now much more in my absence, work out your own salvation with fear and trembling.

May leaders among us ever give commands? In the New Testament we read of many commands from the apostles. I think it is clear that they do command at times. But does Scripture teach us to obey our church leaders? No, it teaches us to obey the truth. In the same chapter where we examined the word for "to obey," I noted that every believer has been given authority to do Christ's redemptive work and to speak the truth; however Jesus forbid us from exercising authority over each other.

Just as Jesus' authority was derived from truth, and not from any position over others, if we are to speak with authority, then what we say must be based on the authority of the truth. Let's look closer at the context of the above two verses where we see Paul expecting obedience. Was Paul bossing the disciples around? Was he the one who called the shots? No! As we have seen in other places, he himself made it clear that he was not. He said he was not a lord over their faith. Rather, the obedience that Paul expected was

not obedience to him, but obedience to the truth and to the gospel!
Let's look at further examples:

Romans 6:16

*Know ye not, that to whom ye yield yourselves servants to
<u>obey</u>, his servants ye are to whom ye obey; whether of sin
unto death, or of obedience unto righteousness?*

Romans 6:17

*But God be thanked, that ye were the servants of sin, but ye
have <u>obeyed</u> from the heart that form of doctrine which
was delivered you.*

2 Thessalonians 1:8

*In flaming fire taking vengeance on them that know not
God, and that <u>obey</u> not the gospel of our Lord Jesus Christ.*

Acts 6:7

*And the word of God increased; and the number of the
disciples multiplied in Jerusalem greatly; and a great
company of the priests were <u>obedient</u> to the faith.*

In the following First Corinthians passage, Paul distinguishes
between advice that was his opinion as an older brother in the faith,
and the command of the Lord. Paul's commands were not backed
by a position over others, but by the authority of the truth. What
Paul commands in this case is basically passing on the command of
Jesus. He says, "I command, yet not I, but the Lord...." While on a
matter about which he does not have the Lord's command, he says,
"To the rest speak I, not the Lord..." He goes on, not to command
what they are to do, but to give his advice as an elder, sharing what
he feels is wise.

1 Corinthians 7:10-16

And unto the married I command, yet not I, but the Lord, Let not the wife depart from her husband: But to the rest speak I, not the Lord: If any brother hath a wife that believeth not, and she be pleased to dwell with him, let him not put her away. And the woman which hath an husband that believeth not, and if he be pleased to dwell with her, let her not leave him. For the unbelieving husband is sanctified by the wife, and the unbelieving wife is sanctified by the husband: else were your children unclean; but now are they holy. But if the unbelieving depart, let him depart. A brother or a sister is not under bondage in such cases: but God hath called us to peace. For what knowest thou, O wife, whether thou shalt save thy husband? or how knowest thou, O man, whether thou shalt save thy wife?

Jesus told his disciples that they were not to exercise authority over others, but he did authorize them to speak the truth. Before he ascended Jesus made it clear that he was giving his disciples authority to pass on his commands to all people and nations.

Matthew 28:18-20

And Jesus came and spake unto them, saying, All power is given unto me in heaven and in earth. Go ye therefore, and teach all nations, baptizing them in the name of the Father, and of the Son, and of the Holy Ghost: Teaching them to observe all things whatsoever I have commanded you.

This is why Paul said, "I command, yet not I, but the Lord...." We should be able to say the same thing about the commands that we give as leaders among Christ's disciples. Apart from the administrative authority which some have over tasks or organizations, I believe the authority which leaders among us have to command is limited to Christ's teaching and to the teaching of Scripture.

Besides the passage in 1 Corinthians where Paul says that it is not really he who commands but the Lord, I found four more places in the New Testament where the word "command" is used in the context of Paul and other leaders commanding the disciples.

2 Thessalonians 3:4
And we have confidence in the Lord touching you, that ye both do and will do the things which we command you.

2 Thessalonians 3:6
Now we command you, brethren, in the name of our Lord Jesus Christ, that ye withdraw yourselves from every brother that walketh disorderly, and not after the tradition which he received of us.

2 Thessalonians 3:12
Now them that are such we command and exhort by our Lord Jesus Christ, that with quietness they work, and eat their own bread.

1 Timothy 4:11
These things command and teach."

In each of these instances, the things that are commanded are actually based on the teachings of Christ or of other Scripture and on the authority of the truth. It could just as well have been stated, "I command, though not I, but the Lord...." If we go beyond the authority of truth or administrative authority in a specific context to assume authority over individual believers, we usurp the role of God in their lives. That is exactly what Jesus warned us that we were not to do!

Some people may still insist that Paul knew he was over others and had a right to order them around. They may quote something like the following, which is addressed from Paul to Timothy.

2 Timothy 4:11-13

Only Luke is with me. Take Mark, and bring him with thee: for he is profitable to me for the ministry. And Tychicus have I sent to Ephesus. The cloke that I left at Troas with Carpus, when thou comest, bring with thee, and the books, but especially the parchments.

I think it's silly to infer from this that Paul was bossing Timothy around. Paul called Timothy his co-worker in both Romans 16:21 and 1 Thessalonians 3:2. He also called him his brother more than once. Do you boss around your co-worker or your brother?

I worked in construction for nine years. When I was working, I would say to my co-worker, "Dave, give me your hammer!" Or he would say to me, "Jonathan, come over here and help me with this!" Was there an inference that one of us was over the other, just because we said something in a command form of grammar? Of course not! We must submit to each other to some degree to be able to work with each other.

I am now living in a different country than where I grew up. I still have some of my things in Pennsylvania. Before my parents fly here to visit me, I might say on the phone, "Mom, bring my Smith Wigglesworth book when you come." Is there any inference that I am over my mother? Of course not! Yet a person who is looking for a *proof* that Paul was over Timothy will infer it from the command grammar used in Paul's request to bring his cloak and parchments.

Submission as Modeled by Jesus

The New Testament does in fact command us to submit to our leaders. I found this in two places, and I also found the command for the younger to submit to the elder. Let's look at these commands and then consider what this submission is to look like by asking how Jesus and the apostles modeled it.

1 Corinthians 16:15-16

I beseech you, brethren, (ye know the house of Stephanas, that it is the firstfruits of Achaia, and that they have addicted themselves to the ministry of the saints), That ye submit yourselves unto such, and to every one that helpeth with us, and laboureth.

Hebrews 13:17

Obey them that have the rule over you, and submit yourselves: for they watch for your souls, as they that must give account, that they may do it with joy, and not with grief: for that is unprofitable for you.

1 Peter 5:5

Likewise, ye younger, submit yourselves unto the elder. Yea, all of you be subject one to another, and be clothed with humility: for God resisteth the proud, and giveth grace to the humble.

As we previously discussed regarding Hebrews 13:17, "Obey them that have the rule over you, and submit yourselves" is better translated as "Be persuaded by those who stand before (lead/serve) you, and submit yourselves." Does our submission to a person imply that they are over us in authority? While in some cases, those we submit to are over us, submission does not necessarily imply the position of one over another. In the sequential reading of the New Testament, by the time I reach these verses, I already know such a thing is out of the question because I know the teachings of Christ that we are all brothers and fellow students—and that we are not to exercise authority upon each other as the princes of the gentiles do.

Notice that in 1 Peter 5:5, not only are the younger commanded to submit to the elder, but all of us are commanded to be subject to each other. Yes, when a person is in authority over us, we submit to them. But that is not at all the only reason we may submit to a person. The fact that we are commanded to submit one to another proves that submission does not necessarily imply the position of one over another. We often submit to people who have no authority over us at all and we do this for various reasons.

Kittel and Friedrich's Theological Dictionary of the New Testament says the following concerning biblical submission:

> *...the general rule demands readiness to renounce one's own will for the sake of others, and to give precedence to others.*[23]

The command to submit to elders does not contradict Jesus' teaching to his apostles that forbade them from exercising authority over each other. Nor does it imply that elders have any authority over each other, or that elders have authority to command based on a hierarchical position over other believers.

When my friends invite me over to their house to eat, and then ask me not to take pizza or soda into the living room because they have a new carpet, do I submit to them? Of course I do! Is it because my friends are over me? No, it is because I am in their house.

We submit to each other so that it is possible for us to work together, or for the sake of harmonious relationships. It's hard to accomplish a joint task with another person when both of you insist on doing it your way! When my family gets together we may want to do different things. I may want to go hiking or do some outdoor activity. My sister may want to go see a movie that I'm not so

---

[23] Gerhard Kittel and Gerhard Friedrich, *Theological Dictionary of the New Testament Volume VIII* (Grand Rapids, MI: Wm. B. Eerdmans Publishing Co., 10th edition, 1984), 45.

interested in. Yet we submit to each other out of our love for one another, and because our relationship with each other is more important than whatever each of us feels like doing at the moment.

Men often submit to leaders who have no position of authority over them but because they are powerful examples to them and influence them. By their words and examples, both Mahatma Ghandi and Martin Luther King Jr. influenced multitudes of people to follow them whom they had no authority over. Eventually even those who formed the policies of nations submitted to them.

I recently read a story from the life of the famous nun, Mother Theresa, which illustrates this well. Mother Theresa dedicated her life to the cause of serving the poor. Some of the most influential and high-ranking leaders in the world sought an audience with her. She gained great influence through love and service.

When Mother Theresa was asked to address a joint session of the United States Congress during the time when Bill Clinton was the president, she spoke about the sacredness of life and the evils of abortion. At the end of her speech, members of Congress spontaneously stood up and gave a standing ovation, while the pro-abortion Mr. and Mrs. Clinton followed suit, standing up and applauding as well.[24]

Although Mother Theresa had no rank in this context, some of the most powerful people in the world submitted to her. Similarly, I believe the leaders of earthly nations will submit to the body of Christ. Yet rank or authority will never gain such submission from those leaders, but it will be gained only by our love, service, and persuasion. Some of those who have the highest ranks in earthly kingdoms will submit to those among us who have no rank but who acquire great influence by Christ-like service.

An even better example of this is found in the story of Bruce Olson, which we will review in the last chapter. Bruce Olson was a missionary who had no rank, and there were certainly very few

---

[24] Darlene (Dee) Parsons, in *In Honor of True Authority*, April 15, 2009. The Wartburg Watch, 2015. http://thewartburgwatch.com

men who endorsed or validated him in any way. He was a perfect example of the slave apostle which we discussed in chapter four. Humanly speaking, he was at the bottom of the barrel. Yet presidents and heads of state submitted to him! It was certainly not a submission that was gained by authority or position over anybody! In fact, although he was a nobody, he was brought before the president of Venezuela and given personal permission from the president to preach the gospel to tribes which were illegal for missionaries to have contact with!

Think of a person trying to help a wounded animal, but because the animal is afraid and doesn't trust that person it fights back. The animal may not get the help it needs unless it submits to the person who is trying to help it. This is the part of the nature of the biblical command to submit to those who stand before us. It is of the same nature as the command to "be persuaded by" our leaders. It is an encouragement to appropriately trust the godly leaders who serve us, to listen to them, and to let them help us.

Often young people do not trust those who are older or value their experience. It is often detrimental to them when they do not submit to the aid of a more experienced person who could help them. But the command to submit to leaders is still no more a command of unquestioning obedience than is the command to submit to one another.

Ephesians 5:21

Submitting yourselves one to another in the fear of God.

Notice that this Ephesians verse does not say "Submitting yourselves to one another in the fear of man." Teaching on submission that is rooted in the fear of man is a perversion of scriptural truth. Teaching on submission that is rooted in the fear of man emphasizes and misuses a few Scriptures exhorting believers to submit to their leaders, but avoids many more Scriptures that teach us to stand for truth and to obey God rather than men. Even though we see the examples of Jesus and Paul doing otherwise, the fear of men says we should not dissent when a leader does wrong, rebuke a wayward leader, or express disagreement with a leader!

Don't forget that the fear of the Lord (not the fear of men) is the beginning of wisdom! Jesus and the apostles learned submission, but it was submission in the fear of the Lord. Because they feared the Lord they weren't afraid to obey God rather than men. We see in Scripture that the fear of the Lord sets us free from the fear of man, enabling us to set our faces like flint and speak the truth just as the prophet Jeremiah did, and just as Jesus did. The fear of the Lord also makes us humble and willing to yield, and careful to relate to others in a godly manner. The Book of James describes this wisdom that is rooted in the fear of the Lord. In the following passage we see what submitting to each other in the fear of the Lord looks like.

James 3:13-17

Who is a wise man and endued with knowledge among you? let him shew out of a good conversation his works with meekness of wisdom. But if ye have bitter envying and strife in your hearts, glory not, and lie not against the truth. This wisdom descendeth not from above, but is earthly, sensual, devilish. For where envying and strife is, there is confusion and every evil work. But the wisdom that is from above is first pure, then peaceable, gentle, and easy to be intreated, full of mercy and good fruits, without partiality, and without hypocrisy.

Submission can sometimes mean having the humility to learn and receive from people from another age, culture, or social status. If submission is based on the fear of the Lord, then it is always submission first to God. When submission is wrongly taught, the fear of man replaces the fear of the Lord. This brings a snare.

Jesus modeled godly submission by looking not to his own needs, but to the needs of others. Jesus modeled submission by laying his life down for others, as opposed to being self-seeking. He yielded his high position and greatness in order to serve the world. He also approached people in the context of their lives and cultures. Paul did the same thing, becoming all things to all men, so as to win some of them.[25] Biblical submission is *honoring*, with each esteeming others as better than themselves. It is putting the needs of others first instead of our own.

Philippians 2:2-8

Fulfil ye my joy that ye be likeminded, having the same love, being of one accord, of one mind. Let nothing be done through strife or vainglory; but in lowliness of mind let each esteem other better than themselves. Look not every man on his own things, but every man also on the things of others. Let this mind be in you, which was also in Christ Jesus: Who, being in the form of God, thought it not robbery to be equal with God: But made himself of no reputation, and took upon him the form of a servant, and was made in the likeness of men: And being found in fashion as a man, he humbled himself, and became obedient unto death, even the death of the cross.

1 Corinthians 13:4-8

Love has patience, is kind; love is not envious; love is not vain, is not puffed up; does not behave indecently, does not pursue its own things, is not easily provoked, thinks no evil; does not rejoice in unrighteousness, but rejoices in the truth. Love quietly covers all things, believes all things, hopes all things, endures all things. Love never fails.

---

[25] 1 Corinthians 9:22

Conclusion

There is authority in the church, but it is not authority of one person over another. The government is on Christ's shoulder. All believers have been given authority to speak the truth, to preach the gospel, to trample on the power of the enemy, and to build up the body of Christ. There are also some among us whom we may appoint to administrative positions, not over people, but over tasks.

We are to command all men to obey the gospel and to turn to Christ. We all, and leaders especially, have a responsibility to rebuke when needed. The Gospels and Epistles have many rebukes from Jesus and from the apostles. Paul told Timothy to rebuke the ones who were sinning.

There are times when we need to rebuke a person who is teaching false doctrine, one who is a troublemaker, or one who refuses to work. However the authority to do this is not based on a position over others, but is derived from the *authority of the truth.* When Paul commanded, he said, "I command, yet not I but the Lord." When Paul did not have a command from the Lord, he gave his counsel. Authority is not given to leaders in the body of Christ to command whatever they think best, but the authority to command is limited to the authority of the truth or to the context of a task over which administrative authority has been given. It cannot be extended beyond that, since the Lord alone is our king and the head of every individual believer.

Submission as Scripture commands is not only to leaders but to each other as well. It is based on the fear of the Lord, and not on the fear of man. Submission as Jesus and the apostles modeled it was certainly not unquestioning obedience to religious leaders, but was a laying down of self-interests for the sake of others. Biblical submission can be manifested as honor, teach-ability, and humility.

Chapter 7
Reactionary Teachings

Reconsidering Teachings that Sounded Good at First

Growing up in a Charismatic church, I often heard references to the importance of "spiritual covering." It made sense to me. I had been very rebellious when I was a child, but when the Lord saved me I got deep into the Book of Proverbs. It was one of my favorite books. Proverbs emphasizes the importance of being teachable and paying attention to the instruction of those who are older and wiser. It teaches us to love correction and warns us against being stubborn and going on in our own foolish ways.

I sought to follow the advice of Proverbs. I repented of rebellion against my parents. As a teenager I tried to learn everything I could from those who had gone before me in the faith. I not only read the Bible through many times, but I also read the stories of heroes of the faith throughout history. I accumulated a collection of Christian teaching books. I read books on prayer and fasting, deliverance, spiritual warfare, inner healing, and other subjects. I loved to read David Wilkerson's sermons. I read books by various YWAM leaders, and also John Sanford, Derek Prince, and many others. I became familiar with the lives and teachings of many people who had been part of the Charismatic movement in the last several decades.

I learned a lot of good stuff, but as I grew in the Lord there was also much that I had to unlearn. It became clear that there were wise and experienced godly men who had very different views about some things, and they couldn't all be right! For example, David Wilkerson's teachings contributed much to my life, but there were a few areas in which he had influenced me that also became a hindrance to me. Later, the Lord used the teaching of Bill Johnson and a few others to straighten me out on those things.

These corrections in my understanding were a form of pruning which resulted in a lot more fruit in my life. I came to have an attitude of being very thankful to the Lord for so many people I could learn from, yet I also saw their humanity and weaknesses. I saw that God had put his treasure in jars of clay!

It became clear to me that there can be a degree of protection in being willing to learn from those with more wisdom, as opposed to being pig-headed and going one's own way. However, as I grew in the faith it also became clear to me that the concept of spiritual covering had to do with much more than just being teachable.

I realized that many things I had heard about spiritual covering were very different than what I understood as I read Scripture. "Spiritual covering" had made sense to me before, because I was once independent to the point of being rebellious. However I began to see that there was also a ditch on the other side of the road.

Yes, many individuals had gone astray because of being unteachable or independent. However, throughout church history whole movements had gone astray by their emphasis on the ideas of what we presently call "spiritual covering." This emphasis was usually an attempt to protect against doctrinal error. Ironically, however, when there was such an emphasis on submitting to a leader, all the people would be subjected to any error that the leader made.

At least, when we were all students with one Teacher, Christ (as Jesus taught), if one person went off the deep end there were others who could provide balance. But when instead, a movement emphasized submission to a person that they saw as their "spiritual covering," those under this "covering" followed the leaders into whatever wrong way the leaders might go. They did not have wisdom to eat the meat and spit out the bones!

I remember seeing the warning in James Chapter Three that not many of us should be teachers, for we all stumble in many ways.[26] And I saw that the context of "we all stumble in many ways" pointed to words and teaching. Was it possible, I pondered, that only the Lord should be our teacher (singular) and guide, while we could yet honor gifts of teaching that the Lord gave in the body of Christ?

Could it be that whenever we subjected ourselves to a person as the one we expected to "cover" and guide us in the way we should go, we would be opening ourselves up to deception by expecting them to fill a role that only the Lord could truly fill? Did not the Lord promise that he himself would be our Teacher, and his anointing would teach us all things?

How could men relate to other believers as their "covering"—those deemed as necessary to guide and protect them—and continue to relate to them as fellow learners and brothers as Jesus taught us? I understood that we have *teachers* in the body of Christ, but that appeared to be a limited role. Did not Jesus say that we all (even teachers) were fellow students? Was this not how we were to relate to each other? When a teacher stopped having the attitude of being a fellow student, didn't that teacher become unteachable and blind to the many ways in which he or she might stumble? It seemed to me that such a teacher then became susceptible to deception along with all of their subordinate "students."

The Shepherding Movement

Such were my thoughts about spiritual covering and teachers. As I considered and discussed these things I was surprised that it

---

[26] James 3:1-2, NIV

seemed so many people had never heard of the "Shepherding Movement."[27] I not only knew some older believers who had been a part of this, but the teaching of some of the leaders of this movement had influenced me. The ones I was familiar with had very good teaching on some subjects, but they also fell into some big errors. This is how it happened.

In the early days of the Charismatic movement, several ministers became very concerned over the moral failure of another minister in Florida. Some of them got together and began to emphasize the need for accountability. They taught that everyone needed to submit himself to another person as his personal shepherd (spiritual covering).

I am familiar with some of these men, who I believe were greatly used by God at times. In the beginning they included Derek Prince, Bob Mumford, Charles Simpson, and Don Basham. They joined together first as the "Holy Spirit Teaching Mission" and later as "Christian Growth Ministries." [28]

Derek Prince and Bob Mumford were both Bible teachers, as was Charles Simpson. Don Basham had a deliverance ministry. Derek Prince had a lot of good teaching, and did healing crusades. I have read books by Derek Prince and Don Basham, and they both contributed to my life. I believe most or all of these men were sincere people seeking God and were at times greatly used by him for the kingdom of heaven.

Nevertheless, when these men joined together in reaction to the moral failure of another minister, they began to emphasize the need for every person to have a personal shepherd. They began to develop a system of safe checks and balances to protect themselves from failure or deception, stressing that everyone had to have

---

[27] The Shepherding Movement, (sometimes called the "Discipleship Movement") was an influential and controversial movement within some British and American charismatic churches. It emerged in the 1970s and early 1980s. Online: http://en.wikipedia.org/wiki/Shepherding_Movement

[28] Holy Spirit Teaching Mission and Christian Growth Ministries. Online: http://en.wikipedia.org/wiki/Don_Basham#Christian_Growth_Ministries

someone he was accountable to. There were pastors who were under them, elders and deacons were under them, and so on until every man had a personal pastor. Last of all were the "sheep." It was a hierarchical pyramid structure.

The more that problems became evident with this setup, the more some began to speak in opposition to the basic tenants of this "shepherding movement." In many ways it began to become a cult even though the intention was to protect people from failure. Submission was so emphasized that leaders were put in the place of God. It eventually had some devastating effects, and even marriages were torn apart by the dynamics of the movement. Often people had to check with their "spiritual father" to get confirmation when they felt God was speaking to them or when they were making personal decisions. It simmered with abuse until finally in 1975 full-blown controversy erupted.[29]

Pat Robertson confronted these leaders and called their teaching witchcraft. Kathryn Kuhlman refused to appear with Bob Mumford at the Holy Spirit conference in Jerusalem. Demos Shakarian of the Full Gospel Businessmen's Association, and many other well know leaders, also opposed them. Pat Robertson wrote an open letter to Bob Mumford saying that their movement was becoming a cult and accusing the leaders of putting their words above Scripture.

The leaders of this shepherding movement at first stubbornly defended their positions, saying the abuses cited were just excesses and the teaching was still all right. They tried to curb these "excesses" in light of the negative publicity they were getting. In spite of their efforts, the teaching and concepts spread, sometimes with altered terminology.

Christian Growth Ministries broke up in 1986. Some of the original leaders later repented, asking forgiveness for their errors.

---

[29] Charismatic leaders including Pat Robertson denounced the Shepherding Movement in 1975, and thereafter voices of criticism continued to swell. Online: http://en.wikipedia.org/wiki/Shepherding_Movement#Criticism_and_controversy

Derek Prince was the first of these, eventually refuting some of the very ideas that he had previously propagated, including the idea of every believer needing a personal pastor.

In 1989 Bob Mumford made this statement about his involvement in the shepherding movement: "I repent. I was wrong. I ask for forgiveness." He also said "Some families were split up and lives turned upside down. Some of these families are still not back together." Bob Mumford admitted that he had not listened to earlier warnings about doctrinal error from others and said, "While it was not my intent to be willful, I ignored their input to my own hurt and the injury of others." He also admitted that there had been an "unhealthy submission resulting in perverse and unbiblical obedience to human leaders."[30]

I began to see what the ditch on the other side of the road was. We are in a dangerous place if we are not teachable and in healthy relationship in the body of Christ. But we also go into error when in reaction to sin or error a human leader is put in a role over the lives of people that should belong only to God.

Ironically, when we or any others are looked to as the "teachers" who should be submitted to and obeyed, we lose teachability, because there is no mutuality. The "teachers" become unteachable. We forget that, as Christ said, we are all students! Obedience to men becomes more important than the love of the truth, and fear of man replaces the fear of the Lord.

If these shepherding guys had such good intentions—yet caused so much trouble that would later bring them to repentance—should we not learn from their mistakes? Those who don't learn from history will repeat it. I don't think the leaders of the shepherding movement wanted to be controlling. The original intention was to avoid failure by keeping everyone accountable. Nonetheless, the fruit of their teaching was control and abuse. We need to be careful that what we teach does not come just from good

---

[30] *Mumford Repents of Discipleship Errors*, Charisma & Christian Life, Strang Communications, Inc., February, 1990, pp. 15,16

intentions, but is Biblically sound. It is important to discover where the truth lies in between the extremes.

Chapter 8
Spiritual Covering

The Role of a Husband to His Wife

What does the Bible say about spiritual covering? Let's start with this passage in 1 Corinthians.

> *1 Corinthians 11:13-14*
>
> *But I would have you know, that the head of every man is Christ; and the head of the woman is the man; and the head of Christ is God. Every man praying or prophesying, having his head covered, dishonoureth his head.*

Here we read clearly what other Scriptures teach—that just as the husband is the head of his wife, Christ is the head, *not only* of the church that is his body, but of every man individually. I have sometimes heard talk about the need for a leader to "provide headship" for individuals in the body of Christ. This is a grave error. Headship has already been provided for every believer—for Christ is the head of every man.

In this verse in First Corinthians, we clearly read that if a man covers his head (Christ) he dishonors his head. That is, we dishonor Christ when we seek other human covering. We also read that the head of the woman is the man, and the head of Christ is God.

This reminds me of a manner of speaking used in the Old Testament. An example is Ruth 3:9 where Ruth asks Boas to cover her with his robe. In a vernacular he would understand, she is asking him to take her as his wife! Husbands, how would you like another man to "cover" your wife? How would you like another man to "provide headship" for your wife? Consider what it is scripturally for someone other than Christ to "cover" or "provide headship for" the bride of Christ: *it is usurping the role of Christ*. It is violating the bride of Christ and sinning against Christ. We could even say it is spiritual adultery.

In ancient times a king would have "eunuchs" who would take care of his harem. A eunuch was castrated so he would not touch the king's women. In the book of Esther we get the picture of the job of a eunuch in preparing the bride for the king.

Leaders in the body of Christ are to relate to the bride of Christ as eunuchs. Their job is to prepare the bride for her groom—for Christ. But they are not to touch her! They are not to put themselves in the place of the groom. They are not to "cover" her or usurp the role of headship!

Protection

Covering can also be talked about in the context of protection, for example:

Psalm 91:4

He shall cover thee with his feathers, and under his wings shalt thou trust: his truth shall be thy shield and buckler.

Deuteronomy 33:12

And of Benjamin he said, The beloved of the LORD shall dwell in safety by him; and the LORD shall cover him all the day long, and he shall dwell between his shoulders.

Chapter 8

Who is our protection? As Psalm 33:20 says, *"Our soul hath waited for Jehovah: He is our rock and our shield."* Scripture tells us in so many places that we must put our trust in the Lord. On the other hand, Scripture also warns us about putting our trust in money, in horses and chariots, in armies, and in man or anything else. To do so is idolatry.

Psalm 118:8-9

It is better to trust in the LORD than to put confidence in man. It is better to trust in the Lord then to put confidence in princes.

Psalm 146:3

Put not your trust in princes, nor in the son of man, in whom there is no help.

Proverbs 29:25

The fear of man bringeth a snare: but whoso putteth his trust in the LORD shall be safe.

Isaiah 30:1-3

Woe to the rebellious children, saith the LORD, that take counsel, but not of me; and that cover with a covering, but not of my spirit, that they may add sin to sin: That walk to go down into Egypt, and have not asked at my mouth; to strengthen themselves in the strength of Pharaoh, and to trust in the shadow of Egypt! Therefore shall the strength of Pharaoh be your shame, and the trust in the shadow of Egypt your confusion.

Jeremiah 17:5-6

Thus saith the LORD; Cursed be the man that trusteth in man, and maketh flesh his arm, and whose heart departeth from the LORD. For he shall be like the heath in the desert, and shall not see when good cometh; but shall inhabit the parched places in the wilderness, in a salt land and not inhabited.

We can see that when covering is used in the sense of protection, the Lord is our *protection*! Certainly there is a measure of protection in listening to sound advice and to the wisdom of more experienced believers. There is a measure of protection in having healthy relationship and fellowship with the body of Christ. Nevertheless, when it comes down to it, only the Lord can be our *protection*! Only he can be our *covering*! Men will fail us; they will lead us astray; they will betray us. God will not! Every believer's trust should be first in the Lord for his or her protection—*not in any leader but Christ!*

Leaders in the body of Christ are to teach others to put their trust in the Lord! We should never desire the faith of others to be resting on us but only on Christ! When we teach people to put trust in man as their covering or protection, they do not develop the intimate relationship they are to have personally with the Lord. We must remember that the role of leaders in the body of Christ is a secondary role, not a primary one. A great problem that we have is that the faith of so many young believers falls apart as soon as one pastor or leader fails them in any way. The more they are encouraged to look to men as their covering, the more evident this problem becomes.

Atonement

Another sense in which the word "covering" is used is that of atonement for sin. The primary word translated "make an atonement" in the Old Testament is "kaphar." This word means "to cover." [31] This seems to be the most common Biblical reference to covering. Atonement covers sin.

The shepherding movement taught that the right thing to do is to obey your leader. However, they taught that you must obey not because the leader is right, but because he (supposedly) has authority from God over you. For example, Derek Prince wrote, "...submission is truly tested only when it requires us to do something we would not otherwise do. Also, as Christians, we do not obey those in authority because they are right: we obey them because they are in authority, and all authority ultimately stems from God himself." [32]

The influence of this teaching often caused people to do things contrary to what they believed God was leading them to do. Many did things that they thought were unwise and even that violated their consciences. They did them because they believed the Lord was testing their submission. The implication was that if in obedience to their leader they disobeyed God or did something they felt was wrong, it was covered by their submission and therefore not counted as sin, but rather as righteousness. That is, they believed they made the right choice by submitting to the "delegated authority" of their leader. One young man said that if he knew that God spoke to him, but his "shepherd" told him differently, he would have to obey his "shepherd" and not God. [33]

I am surprised at how often I hear these same rationalizations today. For instance, when a person in ministry is questioned about wrong or immoral behavior, a typical defense is, "I'm submitted to so and so." The implication is that he is consequently "accountable" and in Gods "divine order," so he doesn't have to answer to anyone else or to the truth. He sees his action as "covered" because he is

---

[31] Word H3722 in *Strong's Hebrew and Greek Dictionaries*

[32] Derek Prince, *Disciples, Shepherding & Authority: A Systematic Scriptural Examination of Controversial Concepts.* New Wine Magazine, 1976, p. 13.

[33] H. D. Hunter, *Shepherding Movement*, The International Dictionary of Pentecostal and Charismatic Movements, Zondervan, 2002, p. 784.

"submitted". In his mind, he is judged not because of his action, but because of his "submission." He has wrongly assumed that if he is *under* someone, he must be in right order.

I have actually heard the suggestion by some well-known leaders today that submission to a person in leadership covers sin. I am shocked that there are many who apparently believe that if they do wrong at the order of a leader they are "submitted to," it is covered and counted as righteousness. They have come to understand this "submission as "God's divine order." It is time for the body of Christ to come to a true understanding that, in the most biblical sense, each believer's "spiritual covering" is Christ's atonement, and not anything else.

The Responsibility We Have For What We Teach

It is important to realize that the problems of the shepherding movement were not only extremes. They were the fruits of erroneous teaching. The way we act is the fruit of the way we are thinking, and the way we are thinking is shown in our words that reflect what we believe and how we have been taught. How do we start with good intentions and get so led astray? It starts subtly. Teachings have very important implications.

We have a great responsibility for what we teach, and especially so when we have great influence. Many believers around the world have learned much of what they practice from American missionaries. American Christian teachers are very influential. I live in Brazil. When I first preached here it seemed people were crazy about hearing an American missionary—to the point that it made me feel a little weird and uncomfortable. The first two times I spoke in a particular church I spoke in English with a translator. The third time, when I spoke in Portuguese, some of the people seemed disappointed that I didn't preach in English!

Because of the sometimes indiscriminate enthusiasm for American "missionaries" and the often less than thorough examination of their teachings, issues that are out of balance or unhealthy extremes in churches in the United States sometimes become even more pronounced in third world countries. It may be that our heart's desire is not to actually control the little details of people's lives but only to guide and protect them, nevertheless doctrine is often developed through a reactionary process that elevates leaders to a role that goes beyond what Scripture teaches. Even if we do not intend such doctrine to be used in an abusive way, as it is passed on it will eventually, almost inevitably, result in abuse.

When we try to keep people on a right path by authority instead of by example, instead of training them to think for themselves and follow the Lord themselves, we make them vulnerable to deception. The fruit produced is believers who feel confused and unable to hear the Lord's voice. They are like prisoners who have been told what to do for so long that when they get out of prison they have difficulty even choosing what to eat. Such control in the name of "protecting" and "shepherding" keeps them from growing up in the Lord. Their faith gets built on men, and when men fail, their faith fails. Cursed is the one whose trust is in man![34]

This is a very serious problem. So many believers who have been "under the covering" of their leaders struggle with feeling as though they can't hear the Lord's voice. They have trouble feeling or believing that the Lord is with them and is protecting them. They struggle with chronic confusion. They have trouble even considering if something other then what their pastor told them is true. They are afraid to believe differently than their "shepherd." They are in bondage to the fear of man. The Lord wants to deliver us from this!

It is not uncommon for believers to be asked, "Who is your covering?" As we have seen, the question implies, "Whose authority are you under?" Jesus was often asked the same question. We will say more about this later, but Jesus' answer was always that he did

---

[34] Jeremiah 17:5

the things that he did by the authority of the Father who sent him. In the same way, Paul emphasized in Galatians that the authority he had did not come from men but directly from God.

Chapter 9
Fathers, Generals, or Brothers?

Fathers and Mothers in the Faith

In First John Chapter Two, the apostle John mentions different levels of maturity in our Christian walk. He writes about little children, young men and fathers.

> *1 John 2:12-14*
>
> *I write unto you, little children, because your sins are forgiven you for his name's sake. I write unto you, fathers, because ye have known him that is from the beginning. I write unto you, young men, because ye have overcome the wicked one. I write unto you, little children, because ye have known the Father. I have written unto you, fathers, because ye have known him that is from the beginning. I have written unto you, young men, because ye are strong, and the word of God abideth in you, and ye have overcome the wicked one.*

In some ways elders in the body of Christ should be like fathers and mothers. Fathers in the faith know the Lord and his faithfulness. Little things upset children, but fathers are a lot calmer. Children easily go astray, but fathers have already made many mistakes and learned from them, so they can warn and admonish children not to fall into the same errors. Mothers nurture and care for little children. Fathers also care greatly about the well-being of children and have affection for them. Both the apostle John and the apostle Paul expressed fatherly affection for new believers.

1 John 2:1

My little children, these things write I unto you, that ye sin not.

1 Corinthians 4:15

For though ye have ten thousand instructors in Christ, yet have ye not many fathers: for in Christ Jesus I have begotten you through the gospel.

1 Thessalonians 2:11

As ye know how we exhorted and comforted and charged every one of you [the Thessalonians], as a father doth his children.

2 Corinthians 2:14

Behold, the third time I am ready to come to you; and I will not be burdensome to you: for I seek not yours, but you: for the children ought not to lay up for the parents, but the parents for the children.

Paul's heart of service toward the saints of the church at Corinth is clearly expressed in 2 Corinthians 2:14. He was not interested in what he could get from them, but in what he could give them. This also reminds me of how he worked with his own hands, personally providing for needs of the young men who travelled with him in ministry, some of whom he affectionately called his "sons."

Chapter 9

Acts 20:34

You yourselves know that these hands of mine have supplied my own needs and the needs of my companions. (NIV)

It is interesting that although Paul was a man, he also expressed a mother's heart towards the young believers. He used the metaphors of a nurse with her children and of a mother giving birth in speaking about how he cared for them.

1 Thessalonians 2:7

But we were gentle among you, even as a nurse cherisheth her children.

Galatians 4:19-20

My little children, of whom I travail in birth again until Christ be formed in you, I desire to be present with you now.

In his writings Paul also spoke of three specific young men—Titus, Timothy, and Onesimus—as his sons. There is one instance each where he calls Titus and Onesimus "son."

Titus 1:4

To Titus, mine own son after the common faith: Grace, mercy, and peace, from God the Father and the Lord Jesus Christ our Saviour.

Philemon 1:10

I beseech thee for my son Onesimus, whom I have begotten in my bonds.

Then, in addition to the Philippians and 1 Timothy examples below, Paul called Timothy his son in 1 Corinthians 4:17 and three more times in the books of First and Second Timothy.

Philippians 2:22
But ye know the proof of him [Timothy] that, as a son with the father, he hath served with me in the gospel.

1 Timothy 1:2
Unto Timothy, my own son in the faith: Grace, mercy, and peace, from God our Father and Jesus Christ our Lord.

In these Scriptures we see the loyalty and love that existed between Paul and a few younger men who worked with him in ministry. Paul loved these men as he would love his own sons.

Call No Man on Earth Father

How do we view these references to "son" if we are reading them in the context of the whole of Scripture? How do we view them in light of our initial understanding when we build on the foundation of Jesus' teaching in the gospels? In that foundational teaching Jesus commands that we call no man on earth father because we all have one Father and are all brothers. It is clear there is an implication of warning in this command. Where is the balance between Paul's fatherly affectionate role and the words of Jesus?

Were Jesus and Paul contradicting each other? No! Jesus commanded that we call no man on earth our father, and we find no place anywhere in the New Testament where a disciple called any human leader his "spiritual father." Even Jesus' disciples did not call him "father." Although Paul expressed the heart of a father and even of a mother towards younger believers, he did not expect them to relate to him as their father, but only to God as their father.

I searched the KJV New Testament for the words that are used in describing how we are to relate to each other as believers. I found the word "brother" used more than seventy times and the word "brethren" used almost two hundred times in the context of how we relate to each other as believers. Many of the instances of this word's usage show how Jesus or one of the apostles related to new disciples.

It is clear that the paradigm of relating to each other as brothers and fellow students applies to the relationships between leaders and new believers just as much as it does to anyone else. Other words that are used in the context of how we as believers relate to each other are "friends" and "co-laborers." For each of the occurrences in the New Testament of "fathers and sons" language, there are about twenty places where we see words like "brothers," "friends," and "co-laborers".

Paul himself used the language of "brothers," "friends," and "co-laborers" when he addressed the churches and also when speaking about the three whom he called sons. "Brethren" was by far the primary word he used in referring to the church family, which he only called his "children" a few times. In Philemon 1:10, Paul called Onesimus his son, but in verse sixteen he called him his brother and also Philemon's brother. He called Onesimus his brother again as well as his co-worker in Colossians 4:9 and 11, and he called Philemon his co-worker in Philemon 1:1

Although Paul referred to Timothy and Titus as his sons, he also called them and other ministers "co-laborers" and "brothers." I found that the Greek word "sunergos," meaning "co-worker."[35] was used eleven times by the apostles in the New Testament in the context of describing how they related to other believers.

Paul called Timothy his "co-worker" in Romans 16:21 and First Thessalonians 3:2, and he called him his "brother" in 2 Corinthians 1:1, Philemon 1:1, and Hebrews 13:23. Paul called Titus his "co-worker" in 2 Corinthians 8:23, and "brother" in 2 Corinthians 2:14 and 8:23. Paul also used the word "co-worker" in describing how he related to the Corinthians.

---

[35] Word G4904 in *Strong's Hebrew and Greek Dictionaries*

2 Corinthians 1:24 (YLT)

Not that we are lords over your faith, but we are workers together with your joy, for by the faith ye stand.

The closer we look, we find with great consistency that the language used in the New Testament is in line with Jesus' teaching in Matthew 23. It shows that in contrast to the leadership in an earthly national government, leaders in the body of Christ are shown on the same level and even under young believers to build them up. The distinction Jesus made between the way we are commanded to relate to leaders in the body of Christ as opposed to secular authorities is consistently found in the rest of the New Testament. Among us, leaders are not rulers, but instead play a part in the Lord's job of shepherding, teaching, and fathering others. In this we see that when we ask believers who their shepherd or spiritual father or teacher is, the answer should be that Christ is their Shepherd and Teacher, and God is their Father

I counted the word "father" used by Jesus in reference to God almost 120 times in the Gospel of John alone! It is used so many times in reference to God throughout the rest of the Old and New Testaments—it was far more then I felt like counting! It is interesting that we never see Jesus himself relating to his disciples as their "spiritual father" or calling them his "sons in the faith." Instead, Jesus said, "I ascend to my Father and your Father" (John 20:17).

Jesus himself, the greatest apostle and leader in all church history, regularly used language of equality in relation to his disciples. He used the words "friends," "brothers," "sisters," and "mothers." Here are a few examples:

Matthew 12:50

For whosoever shall do the will of my Father which is in heaven, the same is my brother, and sister, and mother.

Chapter 9

John 15:15

Henceforth I call you not servants; for the servant knoweth not what his lord doeth: but I have called you friends; for all things that I have heard of my Father I have made known unto you.

Luke 12:4

And I say unto you my friends...

Hebrews 2:11

For both he that sanctifieth and they who are sanctified are all of one: for which cause he is not ashamed to call them brethren.

Romans 8:29

For whom he did foreknow, he also did predestinate to be conformed to the image of his Son, that he might be the firstborn among many brethren.

It is always good to hear sound teaching, yet if we do not read Scripture for ourselves to a greater extent than we listen to teaching, it is very easy to gain a perception of great emphasis on something that is actually a very minor topic in Scripture. We can hear someone preach on the topic of "fathering" and walk away thinking this is a fundamental principle we must adhere to, if we don't understand the full scope of New Testament teaching. We can see the talk in a few places about being a father in the faith, and make "fathers and sons in God's kingdom" the paradigm for how we relate to each other.

Yet, not only is this not the pattern that scripture teaches, it actually contradicts Scripture! When we make these few scriptures describing fatherly affection into *the paradigm* for how we relate to each other, we inevitably violate the paradigm that the New

Testament does emphatically and repeatedly teach, which is that we are all brothers. In the New Testament even Jesus is not called our "spiritual father," but our older brother!

We may frequently hear words in Christian gatherings that are rarely used in the New Testament, or not at all. At the same time, something the Bible strongly emphasizes may be overlooked and entirely lacking. When this is observed, it is a clear indication and a warning signal that we are off balance or going to an extreme on something.

Scripture teaches many things in paradoxes, and it is always best to look at both sides of these coins. Too often Christ's warning to "call no man father" may be sidestepped or neglected when over-emphasizing something Paul said. When we find we are avoiding certain Scriptures, this should show us that we are seeing only part of the picture. It should in turn prompt us to further examine Scripture for a fuller understanding.

Army Language

Besides "fathering" language, we sometimes hear people use army language in speaking about the body of Christ. We hear talk about some being generals, and others being simple soldiers or some other rank. Although the New Testament does talk a little about us being soldiers, it *never* speaks of a hierarchy of command in the body of Christ as in an earthly army.

The idea that the body of Christ is organized like a military hierarchy is a pre-existing mindset that is read into Scripture. It is taking one of the illustrations that the Bible uses in describing our Christian life and employing that illustration beyond the point the writer was making in a particular context. This is how the idea of military rank and hierarchy is inappropriately applied to the way we relate to other believers. When this happens, terms like "generals" for members of the body of Christ crop up which are never used in the New Testament in relation to how we are to relate one to another.

Since the term "general" is *never* used in the New Testament for describing the relationship between one leader and another, and the term "co-worker" is used several times, the term "co-worker" is used infinitely more than the term "general" and should obviously override a military paradigm. The words "brother," and "brethren" are used even more than "co-worker" by a few hundred times—by far the most used in the New Testament in describing how believers are to relate to each other. So why do we let a hierarchical paradigm gain such influence? We may even have wondered, "How can we be an army of believers and not have a hierarchy of command?" Consider this word of wisdom:

Proverbs 30:27
Locusts: they have no king, but they move in formation.

Christ is still the head of every individual believer. We have no human king—only God is our king! God is able to orchestrate his work through every believer according to his will, just as the head of a human body is able to orchestrate the working of each member of the body by sending a signal directly to every individual member. It is essentially unbiblical to think that God speaks to us by passing down orders through a hierarchy of command as is done in an army.

When we make rank in an army our paradigm for relating to other believers, words like "general" become more common, while the words "brother" and "brethren" are used much less—even though they are used hundreds of times in the New Testament! Likewise, we may hear much talk about "spiritual fathers" and "spiritual sons," yet hear very little of the language the Bible actually emphasizes where even apostles relate to other disciples as "brothers" and "friends." We end up hearing much of words and concepts the Bible says little about, while hearing very little of what the Bible speaks a lot about!

Reading Pre-existing Mindsets Back Into Scripture

When we view scriptures written to people in a different cultural context from the perspective and pre-existing mindset of our culture, it is sometimes very easy to read things into them that are not there. It is in this way that people from some cultures often end up compartmentalizing and politicizing what they read in Scripture. Moreover, they may interpret as literal certain vernacular that was intended to be figurative. This is how Paul's figurative use of the words *father, children,* and *sons,* is mistakenly devised into a whole paradigm by which believers are supposed to relate to each other as either fathers or sons.

Next, the supposition that fathers are *over* sons is added to the father-son paradigm when the scriptural admonition: "Children, obey your parents" is applied. Yet in the instance of Ephesians 6:1, the Bible uses the authoritarian word hupakouo̅ (obey), commanding children to obey parents. It's important to note that hupakouo̅ has a very different shade of meaning than the word peitho̅ (be persuaded by) in Hebrews 13:17 that tells us to listen carefully to leaders in the faith. A close look at Scripture shows these kinds of distinctions.

When "fathers and sons" becomes the paradigm we live by, believers become either fathers who are over sons, or sons who are under fathers. This however does not fit in with the whole of Scripture. If we start by first paying close attention to Jesus' words, "Call no man on earth father, for you all have one Father," we will not fall into such assumptions. It is important to understand that the language Paul uses when he calls himself a father and calls others his children is language that is mostly limited to care and affection. It is not meant to identify a paradigm for how we relate to each other in Christ's kingdom. The scriptural paradigm that we have been given for relating to each other is of brotherhood, not "fathers and sons".

When I was in Russia most of the children called me their "uncle." The Russian grandmothers called me their "son." Even in the United States a close friend who is older may call a younger person their "son" or "daughter." In several cultures "father" and "mother" are used as terms of respect towards older people. I am now living in Brazil where the terms "my son" and "my daughter" are used so extensively that even a son or daughter will use them to address their natural parents! I have often heard my wife address her father in Portuguese as "my son" and her mother as "my daughter!"

The way Paul calls those three men "my son" is similar. It shows the affection and care that Paul had for them. These were very close relationships. Paul had been very intimately involved in their lives and had brought the gospel to them. To some degree Paul cared for them as a father would, but Paul was still on the same level with them. He was not their divinely appointed "spiritual father". Just as Jesus related to his disciples as brothers and friends, Paul related to these men as his brothers and co-laborers in Christ. Paul was not their boss and they his underlings. Christ was the head of each one of them. Co-laborer is not a term that you use for your boss but for a fellow worker!

Paul was a helper and an encouragement and example to these men. He was an older brother who exemplified, admonished, and persuaded them of truth, with God alone being the Father whom they were obligated to obey. According to the teaching of Jesus, the natural relationship between a father and his son is *not* the model for the way a disciple is to relate to an elder in the body of Christ. Rather, the natural relationship between a father and his son is a model for the way we all as disciples are to relate directly to God.

It is worth noting that Paul used natural relationships metaphorically in such a way that, if we took him literally, he would be contradicting himself! We should understand that he is using certain relationships as affectionate metaphors, not laying down a paradigm for the way that whole body of Christ is to function. For example, consider the following verses in 1 Thessalonians two:

1 Thessalonians 2:1, 7, 11, 17

You yourselves know, brothers, that our coming to you was not in vain...we were gentle among you, like a nurse tenderly caring for her own children...we dealt with each one of you like a father with his children...As for us, brothers and sisters, when, for a short time, we were made orphans by being separated from you...

Throughout this chapter, Paul addresses the Thessalonians as "brothers" four times. He also uses mothering language in verse 7, and fathering language in verse 11. Finally, he talks of himself as an orphan in verse 17, as if the Thessalonians were his parents whom he had been separated from! So what is it? Is Paul their brother, their mother, their father, or their child? It is clear that figurative language is being employed here.

There are things that we understand from each of these metaphors, however, not all of them can be looked at as paradigmatic for the body of Christ! The teaching of Jesus and the far more extensive use of "brother" language in scripture, makes it clear that the scriptural paradigm for our relationship with each other is of brotherhood. In the same way, it should be clear that the "father and son" relationship is a scriptural paradigm for our relationship with God the Father.

We do not want to make being a "father in the Lord" more than it is in Scripture, but neither do we want to forget that men play a part in the Lord's fathering of us. How do we remain balanced in our approach? How are we to talk about fathering as Paul did, without crossing the line into doing what Jesus warned us not to do in Matthew 23? One way we cross that line is when we overemphasize and assume that every believer needs to have a "spiritual father", giving a "spiritual father" a place in our lives that only God should have.

Chapter 9

Does Every Believer Need a Spiritual Father?

Some who emphasize fathering refer to Moses and Joshua, Elijah and Elisha, and Paul and Timothy. There are certainly things that we can learn from these relationships, yet often insightful questions are not asked: "Who was Moses' spiritual father, Elijah's spiritual father, or Paul's spiritual father?" The assumption that every believer needs to have a "spiritual father" can lead us into several serious problems.

First, when it is believed that every believer must find a "spiritual father," the immediate implication is that they are fatherless if they do not have one! This totally misses the abundance of Scripture pointing conclusively to God as our all-sufficient father. There is much contemporary teaching about "spiritual fathers" that assumes those who don't have a "spiritual father" are lacking, and that those who do not feel they want or need a "spiritual father" have an "orphan spirit," or a spirit of slavery. This kind of teaching misses these fundamental gospel truths Paul gives us in Romans:

> *Romans 8:14-17*
>
> *For as many as are led by the Spirit of God, they are the sons of God. For ye have not received the spirit of bondage again to fear; but ye have received the Spirit of adoption, whereby we cry, Abba, Father. The Spirit itself beareth witness with our spirit, that we are the children of God: And if children, then heirs; heirs of God, and joint-heirs with Christ.*

We may think, "Well, in speaking of the need for spiritual fathers, we didn't mean to say that God is not our father. But we need other fathers too." Is that what Jesus taught? Even as a natural father, if another person believes that my son absolutely needs his "fathering," he implies that I'm not doing a very good job! Sometimes an overemphasis on "fathering" stems from leaders being fearful that God won't do what he said he would do. Yet, God has said he would be a father to each of us—this is foundational to our faith and should give us great assurance.

I have heard several experienced church planters say that one of the most important things they needed to learn was how to let go of people and thereby commend believers to God and to the word of his grace. Paul gives us this precise example in his words to the Ephesians in Acts 20:32. In other words, God led these church planters into an understanding of where their role ended and where they were to entrust the believers to him. It is essential for leaders to trust the Holy Spirit to lead the disciples into all truth. No one but the Holy Spirit can do this! I believe that elders need to know that although they play a part in God's fathering of young disciples, they can never completely fill the role of being a disciple's "spiritual father." This is God's role!

If we teach that every believer needs to find a spiritual father, not only do we go beyond what Scripture says, but we also mistakenly emphasize a need for something that according to the gospel, the believer has already received. It is like constantly telling a young believer they need forgiveness! If they believe that, they are missing what the gospel says about turning to God and receiving his once and for all forgiveness, and so will continue to walk in condemnation!

Likewise if disciples are constantly being told they need a "spiritual father," and they believe it, they are missing the gospel and will continue to feel like orphans. They will believe that they need something they already have in Christ. Young believers do not need to be adopted; rather they need to learn the truth of the gospel, that they have already been adopted and have received the Spirit of adoption.

God is saying to the believer, "You are my son! I have given you the Spirit of adoption. You have an inheritance. I am your wonderful Father." In conflict with this, men are teaching that same person that he is lacking all of these things. When the Christian listens to that erroneous teaching and either doubts or has never learned what he received at salvation, he will have a nagging sense of lack until he recognizes the error and believes the gospel. Recognizing that he already received son-ship, inheritance, and the Spirit of adoption when he was born again will give him assurance to hear and obey God.

When a believer feels that he or she needs to find and be adopted by some elder as a spiritual parent, this interferes with the believer's relationship with the Lord. It interferes with knowing how to relate properly to the Lord and look to God as his or her father.

I have heard of many cases where the idea that believers need to find a spiritual father to adopt them has greatly frustrated those who could not find someone with the time or energy to sow into their lives as Paul did in Timothy's life. Even when they did find someone, they often ended up looking to that person in an unhealthy way. The faith of some began to rest more on their relationship with that person then on the Lord.

Elitism and the Loneliness It Creates

Elitism is typically one dynamic that overemphasis on fathering creates in a group. Some boast by saying for example, "Apostle John Jones is my spiritual father." Others feel like outsiders because they don't have such a wonderful relationship. They feel bereft and lonely. They wish they had a father and an inheritance like the others. They feel like orphans because they don't have someone they can call their "spiritual father."

Then all too often they hear teaching about an "orphan spirit" and think, "That's exactly what my problem is. That's how I feel. I feel like an orphan." This in turn reinforces the perception of need for a "spiritual father." If and when they seek and find a "spiritual father," the relationship that transpires is often not the truly healthy relationship they desired.

For some the relationship is mostly in name. Their "spiritual father" is a person with whom they have little close relationship.

Some "spiritual fathers" will claim hundreds of "sons in the faith," while many of those "sons in the faith" are people they generally see no more than once a year. Some may even pay a yearly fee to be somebody's "spiritual son." Others end up in a relationship that tends to have co-dependence on one side and narcissism on the other. Even if they find a relatively healthy relationship, the emphasis on that person as their spiritual parent can be blinding, causing a tendency to imitate the errors of that person just as easily as the noble characteristics.

If we emphasize and promote fathering beyond what Scripture says, many people end up believing they have an "orphan spirit," when God in his word says they have "the Spirit of adoption." We also forget that Christ is the chief cornerstone. In these ways we lose the healthy dynamic of having various "fathers in the faith," and instead have the unhealthy dynamic of people placing much of their faith on a single human leader.

A wise, experienced, and mature believer who enters a group that emphasizes "fathering" will find it difficult to relate as a "brother" to anyone because of the assumption they are to relate to others as a father or a son. If a certain person is the "spiritual son" of an apostle or other leader, that person assumes he needs to be the "spiritual father" of the new person. In this way, believers are judged after the flesh, and the humble attitude that we are all brethren and disciples is lost. Healthy peer relationships that involve giving and receiving life are very difficult in such an environment.

Heavy emphasis on the idea of fathering may have precipitated from the importance of being teachable and learning from the wisdom of those who have gone before us. What is ironic however is that when everyone is trying to relate to others as either a father or son, being teachable is lost while healthy, mutually uplifting fellowship becomes difficult.

Chapter 9

Frustration of Trying to Relate as a "Son" or a "Father"

I once went through a period where I felt much frustration over this unscriptural emphasis on needing a spiritual father. I just felt like there was no one man whom I could call my "spiritual father." It was not that there were not men who were fathers in the faith to me, because there were in fact several older men who I greatly respected and who had contributed much to my faith. Yet even among the few who had time for a more personal relationship with me, these relationships were only for a season of my life.

Ironically, those who contributed to my life with their wisdom also taught me things I seriously needed to unlearn! In retrospect, I am thankful that my faith was not built on any single person. It was the plurality of these mentors that helped me have a broader perspective.

I was especially grateful for some of these men, but at the same time, I had my own very real and very personal faith in Christ. This faith did not rest on any of these people. It came from Christ and belonged to me! I understood that the greatest of human leaders have many flaws, and I saw the flaws and mistakes of even those I most respected. I saw that God had put his treasure in jars of clay, in imperfect human vessels. I could not call any of these men my "spiritual father." I knew that any or all of them could fail me and my faith would still be intact. I would not be left as an orphan!

In my faith journey, there have been a few people who barely knew me who tried to impose their "fathering" on me to teach me things that I had already *unlearned*. These people were barely acquaintances and knew little of my life—so different from Paul, who had been the very one who brought the gospel to the young men he affectionately called "sons." I honestly felt like these people were trying to get in between Jesus and me and usurp the place of Christ in my life.

People who have learned to relate to other believers as either fathers or sons become accustomed to relating to others with a lack of humility or teach-ability. Because "fathers" approach relationship from a posture of being the "teachers", it is very difficult for them to be teachable or learn from anyone they perceive to be "sons". When the sons look to these men as their "fathers", they all too often accept error because they are not looking primarily to the Lord as their teacher. These assumptions interfere with the working of the Spirit of truth in the people who assume the "father" roles, and those to whom they appeal.

For my part, I can say that I have received from "fathers in the faith," while still only calling God the singular "my father." I feel that to let a person assume that place where I would call him "my spiritual father" would be to violate my conscience before God. I prefer to call those who have contributed the most to my faith "fathers in the faith" and to reserve the term "my spiritual father" for God alone. How could I relate to another believer as my spiritual father when Jesus himself, according to Scripture, relates to me as an older brother?

Similarly, the idea of me being someone's "spiritual father" did not sit well either. Sure, I could sense the father heart of God for younger believers. I was involved in the lives of many people who were younger in the faith, and I cared deeply for them. Yet, even though I at times thought of some of these people as my kids, I did not want them to see me as their father.

For about nine years before I moved to Brazil, I was one of the youth group leaders at a church in Pennsylvania. I became involved in the lives of several young men during that time. I loved these guys! I would hang out with them and have fun, as well as share my experiences in the Lord and try to encourage them to make good decisions and be successful.

I remember when one of these guys came over to my house with his brother late one night after the youth group meeting. He wanted to ask my advice. Since I had to get up at four thirty the next morning to work out of state, I thought I would just encourage the guys and then drive them home. But the Holy Spirit began to move and the young man got very excited and began to pray for everything that came to mind. As he did, winds began supernaturally to move in circles around the room and every time one hit me, I felt the peace of God in the wind. There was no way I could go to bed because of what the Holy Spirit was doing, and so the young men stayed a long time! I finally got to bed at two in the morning hoping for some supernatural sleep!

Some time after that occasion, a pastor friend of mine said to this same young man, "You love Jon don't you? He's your Poppa!" The young man was startled and puzzled. For him the pastor's statement seemed quite out of place so that he blurted out, "My dad? No, that's crazy! Jon is my big brother."

I think it was quite right for this young guy to say that. It was strange for him to think of me as his father. I was only five years older than him. I had more experience with some things then he did and I sometimes gave him advice, but I was just an older brother. I would not have been comfortable with him or any of the other guys calling me their "spiritual father." In fact, what I wanted most for these guys was for them to have their own personal and experiential knowledge of the Lord as I had. I did not want them looking to me as their father or basing their lives on secondhand knowledge from me.

My desire for these guys and for others in whose lives I have been involved is that they know without any doubt that God is their Father and have personal, firsthand knowledge of the Lord. In fact, one of my greatest frustrations in working to build up the body of Christ has been that so many people are living their lives in dependence on a human leader while having difficulty relating directly to the Lord apart from feeling the need for a human mediator. My heart's desire is to always encourage such people while seeking to lead them to direct intimate encounter with God.

I don't want to have people around me who just keep the faith as long as I am with them, but go astray as soon as I am gone like the Israelites did when Joshua and the other elders died. I want them to come to a place where their confidence in God is real and personal so they will not be shaken no matter what any man does.

Identity

Jesus found identity in his Heavenly Father, and we are to find our identity in the same way. Jesus taught us to call God our Father. He taught us that his Father is our Father. Jesus knew that the Father loved him, and he taught us that his Father has the same love for us:

John 17:22-23

And the glory which thou gavest me I have given them; that they may be one, even as we are one: I in them, and thou in me, that they may be made perfect in one; and that the world may know that thou hast sent me, and hast loved them, as thou hast loved me.

1 John 3:1-2

Behold, what manner of love the Father hath bestowed upon us, that we should be called the sons of God: therefore the world knoweth us not, because it knew him not. Beloved, now are we the sons of God, and it doth not yet appear what we shall be: but we know that, when he shall appear, we shall be like him; for we shall see him as he is.

When Jesus commanded us to call no man on earth our father, he was saying that we are not to find our identity in anyone but our heavenly Father. Even if we had a natural father who was abusive and demeaning to us, we are to find our identity in our heavenly Father.

Sometimes leaders in the body of Christ have felt that their job was to be a surrogate father to others, to make up for flaws and bring healing to those whose earthly fathers were absent or lacking. The problem with this is that we still have people looking to an imperfect human being for their identity, and every mistake we make will wound them as well. Rather, it is of utmost importance that we point people to a living relationship with their perfect heavenly Father. For every one of us, it is our heavenly Father's approval that should be important!

John 5:44

How can ye believe, which receive honour one of another, and seek not the honour that cometh from God only!

I would love to be sure that every young man whom I have mentored is so secure in his heavenly Father, so that even if I were to go off the deep end, abandon the faith, or in some way reject them, their faith and identity in their heavenly Father would be intact. Sadly for many, that is often not the case. Innumerable young believers lose their confidence or their trust in God when they see the failure of a leader. Our desire should be that all believers be brought to maturity—to a place where their faith stands even when all around them fall.

The apostle Paul was very concerned about people looking to him in a wrong way. He did not want the believers to find their identity in him. He did not want them identifying themselves as *his* followers. He was a shepherd, but they were not his sheep. They were God's flock. They were not to be his followers or disciples, but disciples of Christ.

1 Corinthians 1:12-15

Now this I say, that every one of you saith, I am of Paul; and I of Apollos; and I of Cephas; and I of Christ. Is Christ divided? Was Paul crucified for you? Or were ye baptized in the name of Paul? I thank God that I baptized none of you, but Crispus and Gaius; Lest any should say that I had baptized in mine own name.

In the same way that Paul lamented, I would feel very uncomfortable to have a young man going around telling everyone,

"I'm Jonathan's spiritual son." I don't mind the affectionate language of a young man saying that an older man is like a father to him, but identifying oneself as that person's "spiritual son" goes far beyond simple endearment.

There is very little difference between a young person saying, "I am Jonathan's spiritual son, and saying, "I follow Jonathan." As Paul expressed, I would likewise be concerned for a young man saying such a thing. My desire would be to guide him to a place of maturity where he finds his identity as a son of his heavenly Father.

I would like to lead every believer to the place where they self-identify as a child of God. I have too often heard young believers identifying themselves as a spiritual son of one person or another, yet rarely or never identifying themselves as a son of God. It is one thing for a believer to recognize a person as a "father in the faith," or even to say that a person is "like a father," but it is altogether different to self-identify by one's relationship with a fellow believer instead of by relationship with the Lord.

Inheritance

There is some teaching about "fathering" that has value, however, I think that the dangers are too often not recognized of extending these truths beyond what scripture teaches. We get into trouble when we make a minor and limited scriptural truth into a major teaching and doctrine. When we take it further than scripture does, we end up contradicting some things that *are* very major and fundamental scriptural truths. For example, the teaching about the need for "spiritual fathers" is often extended to teach specific ways that the role of an elder is thought to correspond to the role of a natural father in the life of a child. Here is one passage that has often been used in this teaching:

Galatians 4:1-2

Now I say, That the heir, as long as he is a child, differeth nothing from a servant, though he be lord of all; But is

176

under tutors and governors until the time appointed of the father.

Some common teaching explains that a young believer, although an heir of everything, has not yet been entrusted with his inheritance. He needs to submit to a "spiritual father" until this "spiritual father" releases him as a mature son to make use of his inheritance. The following Scripture is often used to justify this:

Ephesians 1:18

The eyes of your understanding being enlightened; that ye may know what is the hope of his calling, and what the riches of the glory of his inheritance in the saints.

The reasoning is that our inheritance is in the saints, therefore this inheritance is received by submitting patiently to a "spiritual father" until coming of age as mature sons. This is referring back to the practice of the "placing of a son" that comes from the Greek word for adoption (huiothesia [uiJoqesiva]), meaning to *"place* as a *son*."[36] It is taught that this is the custom of a mature son receiving responsibility and inheritance, and we get it through a human "spiritual father".

They also have emphasized that until that time comes, we are to serve the "father's vision" if we want to receive the "father's blessing" on our lives. It is stated that if we try to come into our inheritance before this time, we are operating out of an "orphan spirit.", because for a son to demand his inheritance before the proper time was a great insult to the father.

However, to interpret this passage in Galatians as speaking of a human "spiritual father" is a gross misuse of Scripture. This passage is clearly speaking of God as our Father, so clearly that it seems an

---

[36] Word G5206 in *Strong's Hebrew and Greek Dictionaries*

attempt to teach otherwise would indicate a lack of integrity in handling the Scripture. Take a look at the following verses:

Galatians 4:3-7

Even so we, when we were children, were in bondage under the elements of the world: But when the fulness of the time was come, God sent forth his Son, made of a woman, made under the law, To redeem them that were under the law, that we might receive the adoption of sons. And because ye are sons, God hath sent forth the Spirit of his Son into your hearts, crying, Abba, Father. Wherefore thou art no more a servant, but a son; and if a son, then an heir of God through Christ.

This passage states very clearly that the time when we were sons who were no different than servants was when we were in bondage under the law! Then it plainly shows that we receive the full adoption as sons when we are born again. We are not servants waiting for a "spiritual father" to release us into our inheritance. We received our "placement as sons", inheritance, and authority from God the Father when we were born again!

The "fullness of time" already came, and it was when we were redeemed from under the law. As Paul in Galatians clearly states, we have already received the spirit of adoption and are not children under the law or servants waiting to be released into our inheritance, but mature sons and heirs of God through Christ.

If we pay attention, we can also see that Ephesians 1:18 does not say that our inheritance is found in the saints. It says that God has an inheritance in the saints! That inheritance is in Christ in us. We already have our inheritance! Christ has revealed to us everything that the Father made known to him, and he has given us the same glory that he received from the Father!

John 15:15

Henceforth I call you not servants; for the servant knoweth not what his lord doeth: but I have called you friends; for all things that I have heard of my Father I have made known unto you.

John 17:22

And the glory which thou gavest me I have given them; that they may be one, even as we are one.

The errors of this misuse of Galatians 4 and Ephesians 1:18 are very serious. Such teaching tells believers that they must receive from a spiritual father that which Scripture teaches God has already provided in Christ at the time of redemption. This is the error that Jesus was warning us against when he said "Call no man on earth father." To deny that believers have received what God has already given through Christ, and to teach that it must be obtained in another way, is to teach a different gospel that is no gospel at all.

The importance of "serving a father's vision", applies directly to God the Father. Contrary to the teaching emphasizing that "spiritual sons should serve leaders," the greatest ones among Christ's disciples are repeatedly commanded to be the greatest *servants* of all. Ephesians says that their job is to "equip the saints for the work of ministry." We see in Acts 20:34 that Paul even financially supported those young men in ministry whom he called "sons," saying in 2 Corinthians 12:14 that children do not store up for their parents, but parents for their children.

Positions of leadership in the body of Christ are not to be places where we find people to support our visions. Rather they are positions where we support others and equip them to fulfill their God-given visions.

This does not mean that young disciples are not to support the visions of elders, because we all are to serve and care for one another. But the elders and the greatest leaders should be the greatest servants. They ought not to be in a position in order to be served or get others working for them. The focus should be to serve others, not hold on to them, but to send them out to fulfill the Father's will. We are to follow the example of Jesus.

Matthew 20:28

Even as the Son of man came not to be ministered unto, but to minister, and to give his life a ransom for many.

Commissioning and Sending

Along with an emphasis on needing "spiritual fathers" on earth, there is also a wrong focus on needing to be sent or commissioned by a human "spiritual father". It is true that if Jesus was sent by his Father and needed his Father's blessing, then we should be sent in the same way. But if we wrongly assume that a man on earth is our "spiritual father," then it follows that we should need that man to commission and send us. It is taught that waiting for this blessing is part of what it means to submit to our "spiritual father."

Yet if we are really living and believing according to the truth that the One who Jesus called "my Father and your Father"[37], truly is our Father, then it is of utmost importance that we receive our commission from God and obey God's command whether or not others are behind us. This is the example that Jesus and the apostles gave. When Jesus was asked by whose authority he did what he did, he said it was by the authority of the Father who sent him.

Some may think that Jesus acted the way he did on earth because he was God. However we cannot forget that Jesus had to obey his earthly parents just like we are commanded to (Luke 2:51). He paid taxes to Caesar (Matthew 22:21). He had to be made in every way like us, and he was tempted as we are (Hebrews 2:17, 18). Jesus was an example for us in everything. We should not think that he just did certain things because he was God and we are not to

[37] John 20:17

follow him in those things. The way that he related to religious leaders is an example for us. He obeyed God even when the religious leaders of his day didn't like it.

We read stories like the one found in Luke 13:10-17 where Jesus was teaching in the synagogue and healed a crippled woman on the Sabbath. The leader of the synagogue was indignant and commanded people to come on the other six days to be healed, but not the Sabbath. Jesus knew that the ruler of the synagogue wouldn't like what he did, but he obeyed his Father in heaven. And when the ruler of the synagogue became indignant, Jesus rebuked him directly. We read in the Book of Acts (5:24-29) that it was in this same way that the high priest, the captain of the temple, and the chief priests tried to put a restraining order on the ministry of the apostles. Yet Peter and the other apostles replied, "We ought to obey God rather than men." (vs. 29)

When we read of ordination and the laying on of hands in the New Testament, we must understand that the purpose of these things is for us to recognize and bless the grace (enablement) of God on a person to fulfill a certain role or task. It is important that we as the church recognize and agree with what the Holy Spirit is doing. At the same time, it is also important that we do not do this foolishly where we put our agreement into what the Holy Spirit is not doing.

The ideal is that we send those whom God is sending, acknowledging God's commission when we lay hands on them and bless them. However when God sends a person, the Bible teaches that they are obligated to obey God whether or not other people recognize or agree with their calling. It is the ideal that elders (as well as others) bless and lay hands on a person who has been commissioned by God, yet even when those leaders who are "acknowledged pillars" do not recognize the grace on a person's life, the Holy Spirit can send ordinary disciples to commission and lay hands on one whom he has called.

The Commission of Paul

Let's look at the life of Paul. In Acts Chapter Nine we read about how after Paul was knocked off of his horse and converted, God commanded a disciple named Ananias to go to him. At first Ananias protested:

Acts 9:13-15

Then Ananias answered, Lord, I have heard by many of this man, how much evil he hath done to thy saints at Jerusalem: And here he hath authority from the chief priests to bind all that call on thy name. But the Lord said unto him, Go thy way: for he is a chosen vessel unto me, to bear my name before the Gentiles, and kings, and the children of Israel.

The Bible does not say that God sent an apostle or any other leader to Paul. Rather it simply says this man was a "disciple" who was sent to commission Paul, and who obeyed the Holy Spirit. Paul also relates the same story in Acts Chapter 22, which includes more of Ananias's words then we read in Acts 9.

Acts 22:12-15

And one Ananias, a devout man according to the law, having a good report of all the Jews which dwelt there, Came unto me, and stood, and said unto me, Brother Saul, receive thy sight. And the same hour I looked up upon him. And he said, The God of our fathers hath chosen thee, that thou shouldest know his will, and see that Just One, and shouldest hear the voice of his mouth. For thou shalt be his witness unto all men of what thou hast seen and heard.

Paul was not commissioned or sent by an apostle or a "spiritual father." He had not yet met the apostles, and the believers were still afraid of him because he had been persecuting them.

Instead, he was commissioned by God and through the obedience of an ordinary disciple who obeyed the Holy Spirit. We see again in Acts 9 that Paul did not hesitate or wait for anyone else's approval but immediately obeyed, before he had met any of the apostles.

Acts 9:20

And straightway he preached Christ in the synagogues, that he is the Son of God.

Paul clearly confirms this in the Book of Galatians. His first words were that he was not sent from man or by man, but from his Father. He then continues to specifically emphasize the same thing. He was speaking as Jesus spoke to those who asked who sent him. Let's take a good look at what Paul says in Galatians.

Galatians 1:1

Paul, an apostle, (not of men, neither by man, but by Jesus Christ, and God the Father, who raised him from the dead)

Galatians 1:11-12

But I certify you, brethren, that the gospel which was preached of me is not after man. For I neither received it of man, neither was I taught it, but by the revelation of Jesus Christ.

Galatians 1:15-20

But when it pleased God, who separated me from my mother's womb, and called me by his grace, To reveal his Son in me, that I might preach him among the heathen; immediately I conferred not with flesh and blood: Neither went I up to Jerusalem to them which were apostles before me; but I went into Arabia, and returned again unto Damascus.

Then after three years I went up to Jerusalem to see Peter,
and abode with him fifteen days. But other of the apostles
saw I none, save James the Lord's brother. Now the things
which I write unto you, behold, before God, I lie not.

Paul makes it clear that he did not hesitate to look for man's approval when God called him. He did not confer with flesh and blood. He was not merely sent by man. His revelation did not come through man, neither was it taught by man. This is a good example for us to follow. We all should have a revelation that was not taught by man.

When Peter said to Jesus "You are the Christ," Jesus answered, *"Blessed art thou, Simon Barjona: for flesh and blood hath not revealed it unto thee, but my Father which is in heaven"* (Matthew 16:17-18). We are blessed when we have a revelation of Christ that comes from our heavenly Father and not merely from man! When the revelation comes from God and not from man, the authority behind it is God's and not merely of man.

We have already read in Galatians 1 that Paul did not even go to meet the apostles until three years after he started to preach the gospel in obedience to his commission from God. Then after three years he finally met Peter. He certainly did not wait for a commission from men in order to fulfill God's calling on his life.

In Chapter Two of Galatians we continue to see the same theme. In the first verse of Chapter Two, Paul states that it was not until fourteen years later that he finally went again to Jerusalem and met the other apostles. Then he actually goes on to say that the apostles and elders in Jerusalem added nothing to him, but rather that God was not impressed with men's positions.

Galatians 2:6 (YLT)

And from those who were esteemed to be something—
whatever they were then, it maketh no difference to me—
the face of man God accepteth not, for—to me those
esteemed did add nothing.

184

Paul goes on to say that these men recognized the grace that God had given to him and gave him the right hand of fellowship. Yet later in verse fourteen, we see Paul opposed Peter to his face in front of everyone. Why? Because Peter was in the wrong!

What is remarkable to me is how I have heard some preach from this very passages of Scripture, saying Paul waited for fourteen years to go into ministry, finally going up to Jerusalem to submit to Peter as his "spiritual father" to be released into ministry by him! How could a person take this passage and use it to teach just the opposite of what it so clearly says?

I believe that there is some good and scriptural teaching about "fathering" in the faith, and not all who teach about "fathering" teach the things addressed here. However when there is such a gross perversion of very clear Scripture where people teach or believe it points to the opposite of what it clearly says, I believe there is spirit of deception involved. It is more than just a mistaken or inaccurate teaching. Again, this was what Jesus warned about when he commanded, "Call no man on earth Father."

Chapter 10
Sent By God

If we are honest with ourselves, a great number of those whom we now consider heroes or reformers in the faith throughout church history follow the pattern of Jesus and Paul. Many of them not only did what they did without needing man's approval, but with the opposition or hostility of the religious leaders of their day.

I have chosen the stories of two modern day apostles whose lives are examples of this to encourage the reader. We can see their struggles and the trials they faced, as well as the victories that followed. Even though they felt the pain of rejection by men and sometimes felt alone, we can see that God never left them. As you read about them, try to think about how you would feel and what thoughts would be going through your mind if you were in their situations. Let their stories encourage you as you see God's faithfulness in their situations.

Bruce Olsen

One of the most striking modern day examples I know that illustrates obeying God in spite of the disapproval and even hostility of religious leaders is the story of Bruce Olson.[38] I first read his story as a teenager. With teenage empathy, I related to Bruce

---

[38] http://www.bruceolson.com/english/english.htm

and imagined what it must have been like to be in his shoes. His famous missionary story is related in the bestselling book *Bruchko*.[39]

Bruce Olsen was a young man who grew up in a legalistic Lutheran church. At a young age he began searching for God. And then, after reading Luke 19:10 when he was fourteen years old, he had a born-again experience. The words that touched his heart were these: *For the Son of Man came to seek and save that which was lost.*

Bruce went on to learn Greek and Hebrew so he could read the Bible in the original languages. As his parents and his church did not encourage him in his faith, he began to attend an interdenominational church. He experienced his first missions conference at the age of sixteen. There he heard a missionary from Papua New Guinea challenge the people to not just give money in the offering, but to go themselves as missionaries. He felt earnestly that God had called him to be a missionary, yet almost nobody took him seriously.

When Bruce applied at various mission organizations, he discovered they all wanted him to go through years of training first. Finally, in early 1961, when he was just 19 years old, Bruce dropped out of college and bought a one-way ticket to Caracas, Venezuela. He left his home, ignoring the protests of family and friends, and landed in Venezuela with seventy dollars in his pocket. He was not sure where he was going to live and did not know Spanish.

Although Bruce had arranged for a missionary to meet him at the airport in Venezuela, the missionary never showed up. After waiting until one-o'clock in the morning, a flight attendant told him that he had to leave because the airport was closing. Since he would need to get a hotel room, Bruce skipped breakfast and lunch

---

[39] Bruce Olson, *Bruchko: The Astonishing True Story of a Nineteen-Year-Old's Capture by the Stone-Age Molitone Indians and the Impact He Had Living Out the Gospel among Them.* (Strang Communications. now Lake Mary, FL: Charisma Media, 1995).

the next day to save money. He was hungry, alone, almost out of money, and had no place to go.

The following day, a young college student named Julio began to talk with Bruce in broken English and invited him to stay with his family. He was glad to accept, and began to learn Spanish as he stayed with them. After some time Julio introduced Bruce to a doctor who was willing to take him to meet some natives and visit a jungle missionary compound.

Bruce was hoping to find Mr. Saunders, the missionary whom he had expected to meet him at the airport. He was sure that Mr. Saunders would be friendly and apologize for forgetting to meet him. Instead, Mr. Saunders' response was, "What makes you think you can come to South America without a mission agency? You just want to come down and impose on us. You think we'll have to take care of you. But you're wrong. You're on your own, Buster." The other missionaries at this compound were also extremely closed toward Bruce.

Soon after returning from the jungle, Bruce befriended two young guys, Bob and Tom. They were some of the missionary kids and were close to his same age. It felt good to finally speak English again after several months of struggling to communicate in Spanish. After hanging out and having a good time, Tom said, "I wish you could come for dinner, but my dad, well...he wouldn't."

Bruce longed to be with friends, but had nowhere to go. When he didn't see the guys on the street the next day, he went to the mission station to find Tom. Tom came to the door looking embarrassed. He explained that he was no longer allowed to see Bruce. Tom explained, "My father says that you've been put out of fellowship. That means none of the missionaries are supposed to greet you."

Bruce was shocked and surprised, and asked why he had been put out of fellowship. Tom responded, "You won't obey them. They told you to go back to the States, join the mission, and then come here and work." Bruce asked, "How could I even get back? Will they buy my ticket? And since when do I have to obey their orders?" Tom's only explanation was, "I don't think I should talk to you about this any longer. Goodbye."

I can imagine how many of us would have felt in Bruce's predicament. Most of us would have probably been bombarded with thoughts of doubt and regret. Imagine being in another country without a return ticket, away from all friends and family, broke, and relying mostly on the hospitality of poor families. Think of the frustration and discouragement Bruce must have felt in not yet knowing the language. Imagine experiencing the rejection of those he thought would encourage him as he learned they thought he hadn't "obeyed" them. Did he *miss it* when he thought God sent him to Venezuela? Yet Bruce kept hearing God say to him, "Although everyone else may forsake you, I will not forsake you."

One day as Bruce was facing the problem of getting a visa to stay in the country, he sat down at a table in a crowded restaurant. A stranger sat next to him. When Bruce began to talk with the man and tell him about his predicament, the man offered to help. This man was Roberto Irwin, private secretary to Rómulo Betancourt, who the president of Venezuela! Yes, Roberto was able to help him to get a visa.

As he was living in Venezuela, Bruce heard about a tribe called the Motilones and felt that the Lord was telling him to go to them. They lived on the border of Columbia and Venezuela and were known for killing every white person they came in contact with! They had had very little contact with the outside world, and not much of their culture was known. Bruce began to learn all he could about them and applied to the government for a permit to contact native peoples. His appeal for a permit, however, was repeatedly rejected. Missionaries were unwanted.

When Bruce prayed, he felt that the Lord told him to contact Roberto Irwin again. Roberto introduced him to President Betancourt. Finally, Bruce was able to tell his story to the president. When Betancourt heard his story he granted Bruce personal permission to work with any tribe in Venezuela.

Chapter 10

The Motilones

The Motilones believed in one God and also believed in spirits. However, they believed that God had rejected them for deceiving him. Yet, they had a prophecy of hope that a tall man with yellow hair would come to them with a banana stalk, and God would come out of the banana stalk.

When Bruce set out in the jungle searching for the Motilones, he first met another tribe, the Yukos. They thought he was crazy for wanting to meet the dangerous Motilones, but he kept moving closer to them. Bruce's first Motilone encounter was a five-foot arrow in his thigh. He was captured and his wound became infected. He became very sick with amebic dysentery and escaped at night. After fifteen days of wandering through the jungle without food, he managed to find his way back to civilization and get medical care.

After just two weeks of recovery, he quickly set out to find the Motilones again. He brought a canoe full of medical supplies and gifts, which he left on their trails. For months the items were undisturbed, but then he found them gone and replaced by four arrows in the trail. This was known to be a warning meaning to stop or die! Still he continued. He was greeted with drawn bows again, but this time Bruce recognized one man from his first capture and he gave the Motilone greeting. This familiar Motilone then spoke to the others and they lowered their bows. After this, Bruce was free and was treated with curiosity. He began to learn their language and culture.

When he set off with some of the natives to meet the chief, he became very sick with hepatitis. The Motilones carried him the rest of the way to the chief, and he was almost unconscious when he got there. The chief was going to execute him, but was persuaded that he couldn't execute such a sick man who was going to die anyway. Then rescuers in a helicopter found Bruce, and he again made it back to civilization to get the needed medical help. After a few weeks of recovery, Bruce returned yet again to the Motilones.

It took years of living with the Motilones for Bruce to learn their language and culture. He began to introduce modern medicines and sanitation principles. It was a long time until he could even begin to think about sharing the gospel with them. He became a part of their society and became best friends with the man whose arrow had first hit him.

At first some of the Motilones had wondered if he might be the tall man with yellow hair from their prophecy, but they figured he couldn't be because he didn't have a banana stalk. But one day in 1965 Bruce's best friend, Bobarishora, cut open a banana stalk, and the leaves inside spread out like the pages of a book. Bruce pointed to his Bible and said, "This is God's banana stalk!" He explained that the Bible has words that tell us about God. He then used a Motilone legend to explain the gospel to his friend.

Bobarisha realized that Bruce really must be the tall blond man carrying a banana stalk, and he accepted the message with joy. Bruce was amazed at the new joy and peace that he saw in his friend's life. He was, however, frustrated because Bobarishora would not share his new faith with anyone else! Bruce didn't realize how important it was in the Motilone culture to wait for the right time to share something so important.

Bobarishora knew the right time. The Motilones would have big communal festivals with feasting and singing contests that lasted for hours. The contests consisted of singing stories of all of the important news. At the next big festival, Babarishora sang a fourteen-hour song that communicated the story of Christ and the message of the gospel to the other Motilones. The tribe as a whole decided that they wanted to follow Christ. It was indeed the right time!

Bruce continued to translate the Scriptures into the Motilone language, and taught the tribe to read. He has worked tirelessly for the welfare of other tribal groups too. The Motilones soon sent missionaries who evangelized the surrounding tribes, while Bruce proceeded to learn the languages of those tribes.

Bruce became an advocate for the natives, working to protect their land rights. He became very influential because of his efforts to help the people who God sent him to. He has been friends with five Colombian presidents and has spoken before the United Nations. His story is famous as an example of bringing the gospel to a people group and preserving their culture.

He introduced domesticated animals and crops so that the Motilones could have a more stable life and food supply. He built facilities and trained native people to work in eighteen health centers, forty-two bilingual schools, twenty-two agricultural centers, and eleven trading posts that operate as co-operatives. The co-operatives, which are self-sufficient, not relying on outside help, sparked social development in places overlooked by the governments of Colombia and Venezuela. They provide the economic base for eighteen tribal peoples.[40]

Many times as Bruce pursued his ministry to these people, he endured hunger, discouragement, and sickness. Because authorities of the religious establishments around him did not recognize that Bruce was not sent by man but by God, they did not bless him, but instead opposed him. Nevertheless, Bruce ended up learning the culture of the Motilones and evangelizing them, eventually learning over twenty languages and evangelizing many other native tribes as well.

Bruce went on to become an advocate for the natives and a very influential person in the nation to which he was sent. Later he was even kidnapped because of his influential status and tortured by communist guerrillas. Even so, before his release, many of those terrorists came to Christ. The presidents of both Columbia and Venezuela shook hands with him when he was returned.

---

[40] *Legacy* at http://www.bruceolson.com/english/english.htm

Loren Cunningham and YWAM[41]

Loren Cunningham was about twenty years old when in the Bahamas he had a vision of the world with waves crashing on the shores of all the continents. The waves went up higher each time until they covered all of the land. As he continued to watch, the waves became young people everywhere going from house to house, preaching the gospel, and caring for people.

Within the next few years Loren was ordained in his denomination and received a good job as a leader of youth activities. However, he felt like many of the activities were really meaningless. Remembering his vision, he received approval to take 106 young people on a mission trip to Hawaii. The trip was a great learning experience for him, teaching him how to plan and manage future trips.

As Loren reflected on his vision and observed himself making mental notes of his experience leading youth on missions, he felt the need to act. He sold his car in order to be able to take a trip around the world and scout out the possibilities for evangelism overseas. As he traveled, he was deeply affected by the needs of people around the world. When he returned to the United States, he toured the country, telling young people about his international experiences. At that time, however, he didn't have a way to engage their involvement.

Loren realized that one of the biggest obstacles to these young people reaching the world was that the present system required years of prior schooling. He saw that by the time young people got through school, most would forget their fiery zeal. He could no

---

[41] The story of Loren Cunningham and Youth With A Mission (YWAM) is found in the book *Is That Really You, God?* By Loren Cunningham and Janice Rogers, YWAM publishing, 2001

longer challenge young people to change the world when there was no channel for them to do so.

Motivated by the desire to open a path for young people, Loren and some friends started *Youth With A Mission*[42] in 1960. Loren converted his bedroom into an office and YWAM began to receive volunteers who would each pay their own way to serve on short-term mission trips. Loren's father soon let him know that some leaders in their denomination were quite unsupportive of the idea of sending young people with minimal training on mission trips. In response, Loren decided to meet with the people in his denomination who were in charge of missions.

The denomination leaders were quite concerned with the problems that sending young and inexperienced people as missionaries might cause, and the dangers that they would face. They were already having difficulties with keeping experienced missionaries in the countries where they served. Seeing Loren's discouragement, one man suggested the option of sending out vocational volunteers to mission compounds that were well established.

Loren liked the idea and went with it. The first young YWAM missionaries were two young men who were heavy equipment operators. They went to Liberia for a year to work on building a road to a leper colony. With this success, more trips to other locations followed.

YWAM soon recruited 146 young people to go on an eight-week trip to the Bahamas and the Dominican Republic. The goal was to bring the gospel to every household in the islands of the Bahamas. The trip was very successful, and the young people shared wonderful stories of miracles and salvation. Not only that, the youth were impressive evangelists: about six thousand people had shown interest in following Christ, and two churches were planted. Loren and his wife returned with joy, excited to tell the

---

[42] Youth With A Mission, YWAM History, Youth With A Mission Worldwide Website, Online: http://www.ywam.org/about-us/history/

leaders back home what God had done through the young people on their trip.

Back in the States, Loren had a meeting with the superintendent of his denomination. He anticipated a very positive response to the success of the mission. Instead he was told that new works like his had to be brought under the denominational umbrella and could not remain autonomous. This was a major problem for Loren, as YWAM had been opened to young people of *all denominations.*

The denomination went so far as to offer Loren a good job with a great salary, staff, and budget. He would be allowed to continue his vision, but only in a limited way. He could take just ten to twenty people a year on mission trips. Loren understood that the offer was very gracious, but it was not what God had called him to do.

God had given Loren a vision of waves of thousands of young people of all denominations going out and evangelizing all over the world. Though he tried to explain this, he was left with the option of either following the denominational rules or resigning. Feeling that he must obey God, he shook hands with the superintendent, thanking him for the offer, and resigned.

It was a very painful and difficult choice, leaving Loren confused. He realized that people would think that he was kicked out and his reputation could be hurt. The pain of rejection affected Loren, and although he was determined not to rebel, over time bitterness settled in his heart. Later while fasting and praying Loren realized he had to repent and reconcile with those who did not support the vision God had given him.

Today YWAM has thousands of full-time missionaries and has reached many millions of people around the world with the gospel. What accounts for this success? Loren was not sent by men, but by God. Today, people see the incredible fruit that has come from YWAM and recognize that it was necessary for Loren to leave his denomination in order to obey the Lord. However, even many now recognize the great fruit of Loren's obedience to God, but continue to rebuke those who are attempting to obey God instead of man, as Loren did. What would they have said to Loren about disobeying his pastor's vision if they had been a part of what happened in the formational days of YWAM? Would they not have rebuked him as well?

Yes, many would have said that Loren should submit to serving his pastor's vision and not insist on doing things his own way. They would see him as young and rebellious, going out on his own, with no spiritual covering, and with an "independent spirit". However, if Loren had believed such accusations, it is likely he would never have fulfilled the calling of God upon his life.

What can we learn from their stories?

I wanted to give some practical modern examples of people who have obeyed God even when they faced the resistance of religious leaders. While I've given just two, they have much in common with the stories of so many whom we see as heroes of the faith throughout Christian history. These are stories of people who had to look to the Lord and obey God when men failed them.

Obviously what we see in their stories is not the ideal. The ideal would have been the church and leaders around them recognizing what God had called them to do, laying hands on them, praying for them, and helping them. Nevertheless, in their stories we see examples of obedience to God even when abandoned by men. We see the struggles and discouragement they faced and the victories that finally resulted.

Bruce was weak and unimpressive by the standards of what many might consider a good candidate for an apostle. Almost nobody took him seriously or even noticed him, and he didn't fit into anybody's mold. Neither did he have the training or qualifications that others believed he needed. He was just a kid. He didn't have the experience or training of "wiser" men who had decades of experience in missions.

Most people might think what Bruce did was foolish—flying to Venezuela with almost no money or support, without knowing the language; and it certainly might have been foolish if God had not called him to do it!

As leaders and fellow believers, we need to be sensitive to the Holy Spirit so we recognize when God is calling somebody to something that would not normally seem to make sense to us. In this way we can encourage them. We should desire to see what God is blessing so that we can join our blessing with God's. Someone may not have the conventional training to fulfill a task or seem like the person for the job to our natural eyes, but we must remember that God chooses the foolish things of the world to confound the wise.

It should humble us to recognize that even though God calls us to agree with his purposes and to lay hands on those whom we recognize the Holy Spirit has set apart, their call and release never depends on us or on our sending, but on God. It will however make it a lot easier for those who God sends if we agree with God in sending them. Even though Bruce didn't have the encouragement or blessing of leaders in his life, and even though nobody recognized his call, God still called him. God still blessed him and promised to never leave him.

Sometimes Bruce may have felt as though God was not with him, such as when the missionary who promised to meet him at the airport abandoned him, never showing up. That man later even opposed him. Bruce was thousands of miles from friends and family, in a country whose language he didn't speak, without a way to return home. He didn't have any money or place to go! Imagine the voice of the adversary whispering in his ear, "See, you hard-headed, foolish, rebellious young man! You didn't listen to your leaders, and now this is what is happening to you! You came out from under their covering, and now you have lost your blessing! You blew it!"

But instead, the Lord kept telling him, "Even though all may abandon you, I will never abandon you."

Bruce had a difficult path to follow. He longed for friendship, but when he finally started to make a few friends, an older missionary rebuked him, telling him to go home or submit to their way. Because he didn't obey them, he was put out of fellowship and ostracized. He had almost no Christian fellowship, and nobody to talk to. He certainly had no "spiritual covering" except for the blood of Jesus and the glory of God the Father. And imagine how much more difficult the further trials he was about to face were without the friendship and encouragement of other believers!

In the same way, God had a difficult path for Jesus to follow. When Peter rebuked him, Jesus stood his ground and said, "*Get thee behind me, Satan: for thou savourest not the things that be of God, but the things that be of men*" (Mark 8:33). In the same way people who are thinking according to earthly wisdom may rebuke us when we seek to obey God. Satan will try to discourage us by reminding us of their words, trying to get us to think that their rebuke must have been from the Lord after all, and that we made a mistake.

It is important that when the Lord sends us, we stand firm. We must remember that often when we follow the call of the Lord we will face impossible situations. We learn to rely on God's power when we face things that are too difficult for natural ability. As Bruce did, we must remind ourselves of God's promise—that he would be with us always, and would never leave us or forsake us.[43]

For many years Bruce didn't even see one convert, but in the end there was an abundant harvest. Multitudes thank God today for Bruce's obedience and perseverance!

Likewise, the story of Loren Cunningham and YWAM is a good example of when human advice that sounds wise would detract us from obeying God. Although Loren's leaders were opposed to him doing exactly what God had led him to do, they offered him a great job, and a good salary. He would be able to fulfill a little part of what God had told him—he could take out ten

---

[43]Hebrews 13:5

or twenty young missionaries a year. What if he had thought this was God's way of teaching him to wait until he was ready, and to just be faithful with the small things for now? But Loren didn't compromise. He obeyed God.

There was nevertheless a cost for obeying God, and part of that cost for Loren was losing the support of people who he had grown to love, some of whom he may have looked up to. Part of that cost was also suffering disgrace, because he knew that many people would think that he had been fired. The pain of rejection settled in his heart, and he became bitter. He finally realized how much this bitterness was hurting him and that he needed to repent.

We might experience something like this when people do not recognize the call God has given us or otherwise support us. Why does it hurt so much when leaders are not on board with our vision? Most likely it is because we desire people's approval, while on the other hand fear of the Lord makes us secure in God's approval. We must let the fear of the Lord set us free from the fear of rejection. We have to let go of any hurt. God's desire is that we obey Him and forgive others so we don't allow a root of bitterness to grow in our hearts.[44] Bitterness will not be able to take root in our hearts over the rejection if it is the Lord whom we seek to please, and not men.

I want to point out that following the Lord even when leaders do not support us is very different from becoming proud and independent. Even after Loren left his denomination, he continued to listen to and learn much from older and more mature believers. It is dangerous to reject wise counsel or to think that we do not need to receive from older and more mature believers. However we should not unquestioningly obey our leaders, but rather listen carefully and respectfully to them and consider if God is speaking to us

---

[44] Hebrews 12:15

through them. It is important that we remain humble and teachable.

Another powerful and similar story is that of John Wesley, whose influence changed a nation and the course of history. Wesley's obedience to God was a key factor in the abolition of slavery. Though his ministry began in the Anglican Church, as time went on, Wesley was persecuted by the Anglican Church because he sent out preachers who were not officially ordained—men not approved by man, but by God. Wesley later ordained preachers in the United States without the approval of the Anglican Church. At times he faced intense opposition, mobs, and violence.

It has been observed that people who participated in a previous move of God often end up persecuting those who are part of the following one. This should help prepare us to forgive those who don't understand, while we yet obey God when we know that he has sent us; and then, as we mature, to remain humble and ready for what God is doing in the next generation. In this way we will be ready to say "Amen" to what God is doing instead of persecuting those carrying on God's call.

Final Prayer

Heavenly Father, thank you that you are our Father! Thank you that you have given us everything that we need for life and godliness in the knowledge of our Lord and Savior Jesus Christ! Just like Solomon did, we ask for your wisdom, the wisdom we now know is Christ in us to lead in a way that truly represents you and your kingdom—being confident that you will answer us!

We thank you for the abundance of grace that you supply when we face difficult circumstances and choices. We ask you to guard our hearts and keep us from straying either to the right or the left.

We forgive those who have wronged us, hurt us, or misled us, and pray as Jesus did, "Father, forgive them, for they know not what they do." Thank you Holy Spirit, for healing our hearts, for building us up in the knowledge of you, and for training us to renounce ungodliness. Thank you for strengthening our hearts and filling us to overflowing with the love of God! We receive all of the grace that you have made available for us!

Thank you for teaching us to fear you and for delivering us from the fear of man! Help us to stick to the course that you have given us no matter what! Thank you for establishing us so that we are "firm, unmovable, and always abounding in the work of the Lord!"[45]

Thank you Father for the tremendous privilege of serving others along with you, just as Jesus serves us! Thank you for leading us to repentance and teaching us evermore how your wonderful heavenly kingdom functions. Thank you for your grace resting on us in power, and for enabling us to help and to serve, to rebuke and to admonish, to encourage and to build up, and to lay our lives down for those whom you have entrusted to us.

Amen!

---

[45]First Corinthians 15:58

Bibliography

Accordance Bible Software—Bibles: English Standard Version, King James Version, New American Standard Version (95S), Young's Literal Translation. Version 9.6, Oaktree Software Inc., Tulsa, OK: August 2012.

Baker, Heidi and Rolland, ministry website— *https://www.irisglobal.org/* Amazon Author Page— *http://www.amazon.com/Heidi-Baker/e/B001JP8H7S/ref= sr_tc_2_0?qid=1433795475&sr=8-2-ent*

Barna, George, The Fuller Institute, and Pastoral Care Inc. *http://www.pastoralcareinc.com/statistics*

Charisma and Christian Life, Strang Communications Inc., February 1990 *Mumford Repents of Discipleship Errors*

Cunningham, Loren and Janice Rogers *Is That Really You, God?* YWAM Publishing, 2001

Dodd, Brian J. *Apostles, Slaves of Christ.* Online: *http://www.harvest-now.org/fileadmin/resources/en/friends/ Apostles%E2%80%94Slaves_of_Christ.pdf*

Examiner.com *http://www.examiner.com/article/mongolia-from-2- to-50-000-christians-20-years*

Helps Ministries, Inc. *HELPS™ Word-studies* copyright© 1987, 2011 www.HelpsBible.com

Hill, Stephen W. *http://www.harvest-now.org/nachrichten-der- ernte/n/?L=3%27%22&tx_ttnews[tt_news]=269&tx_ttnews[yea r]=2008&tx_ttnews[month]=12&tx_ttnews[day]=03&cHash=f2 e0af8acb037c4963bd7d578648f193*

Hogan, Brian online interview
    https://www.youtube.com/watch?v=MHboMIEPxAo
Hunter H. D—*Shepherding Movement, The New International
    Dictionary of Pentecostal and Charismatic Movements*,
    Zondervan, HarperCollins Christian Publishing, Nashville, TN:
    May 2002.
Kittel, Gerhard and Gerhard Friedrich—*Theological Dictionary of
    the New Testament Volume VIII*. Grand Rapids, MI: Wm. B.
    Eerdmans Publishing Co., 1984.
Moulton, James and George Milligan *The Vocabulary of the Greek
    Testament* Hodder and Stoughton, 1963. London, England
Olson, Bruce. *Bruchko: The Astonishing True Story of a Nineteen-
    Year-Old's Capture by the Stone-Age Molitone Indians and the
    Impact He Had Living Out the Gospel among Them*. Strang
    Communications, now Lake Mary, FL: Charisma Media, 1995.
    Story Online: *http://www.bruceolson.com/english/english.htm*
Parsons, Darlene (Dee)—*In Honor of True Authority*, April 15,
    2009. The Wartburg Watch, 2015. Online:
    http://thewartburgwatch.com
Prince, Derek—*Disciples, Shepherding & Authority: A Systematic
    Scriptural Examination of Controversial Concepts*. New Wine
    Magazine, February 1976. Online:
    http://www.csmpublishing.org/pdf/newwine/02-1976.pdf
Strong, James—*Strong's Exhaustive Concordance*.
    BibleStudyTools.com, Salem Web Network. Online:
    http://www.biblestudytools.com/concordances/strongs-
    exhaustive-concordance/
Vance, Dr. Laurence M. *A Brief History of the King James Bible*
    Vance Publications, Pensacola, Florida. Online:
    http://www.av1611.org/kjv/kjvhist.html
Vine, W.E. *An Expository Dictionary of New Testament Words
    Volume 3*, Oliphants Limited, 1946
Wikipedia *Online: http://en.wikipedia.org/wiki/Don_Basham#
    Christian_Growth_Ministries*
Wikipedia *Online: http://en.wikipedia.org/wiki/Rosa_Parks*

Wikipedia *Online: http://en.wikipedia.org/wiki/Shepherding_ Movement*

Wikipedia *Online: http://en.wikipedia.org/wiki/Shepherding_ Movement#Criticism_and_controversy*

Recommended Reading

Always Enough: God's Miraculous Provision among the Poorest Children on Earth, by Rolland and Heidi Baker

Compelled by Love: How to change the world through the simple power of love in action, by Heidi Baker

Birthing the Miraculous: The Power of Personal Encounters with God to Change Your Life and the World, by Heidi Baker

There's a Sheep in my Bathtub: Birth of a Mongolian Church Planting Movement, by Brian Hogan

Bruchko: The Astonishing True Story of a 19-Year-Old American, His Capture by the Motilone Indians and His Adventures in Christianizing the Stone Age Tribe, by Bruce Olsen

Is That Really You, God? Hearing the Voice of God, by Loren Cunningham and Janice Rogers

About The Author

Jonathan Brenneman was born in Rochester, New York and raised in Pennsylvania. Although a very troubled child he was at the same time very religious. He read the Bible from cover to cover when he was seven years old, all the while questioning and wondering about the existence of God.

When Jonathan was nine years old, he woke up one morning with bad back pain. His mother prayed for him, and to his surprise, he felt something like a hot ball of energy rolling up and down inside his back, and the pain melted away. It was shocking to say the least, but it convinced him God did exist! He later told his friends, "I know that God is real. I felt his hand on my back."

In spite of this experience however, Jonathan still had no peace. He prayed the "sinners prayer" but with no change until two years later when he had a "born again" experience. It felt like heaven opened and unexplainable joy and peace descended upon him! He was different, and knew it! The things he had felt so guilty about that he tried unsuccessfully to change, were simply gone.

After this time, Jonathan dedicated his life to the Lord as a missionary, going on his first mission trip at age fourteen. As a teenager and young adult he continued to travel and learn languages. Then, when he was twenty-one and during a time of desperation, Jonathan went to a Christian conference where he was very encouraged and touched by the Lord. It was a start of a supernatural lifestyle and growing in spiritual gifts during which time many amazing miracles and healings began to happen.

Jonathan worked in construction, but in between jobs he began to visit churches in the United States and Canada as well as in Latin America and Eastern Europe. His ministry journeys have included Russia, Ukraine, Poland, Italy, Canada, Mexico, Belize, and Brazil. In these places Jonathan has encouraged the believers and shared testimonies, and spoken with unbelievers and prayed for them. He also worked with children and seniors. He dedicated a lot of time to talking with, praying for, and encouraging people wherever he went, all the while growing in an experience of a love for people that is beyond understanding—for it is God's love. Jonathan believes it is a wonderful and tremendous privilege to be able to serve the people for whom Jesus gave his life.

Jonathan now lives in Rio de Janeiro Brazil with his wife Elizabeth, and baby daughter Rebekah. He loves people very much, enjoys being with them, and rejoices at seeing what the Holy Spirit does in their lives. He likes to minister in the role of caring for people, laying hands on the sick, visiting the elderly, and working with children—always with the intention of loving them so they in turn will learn to love others with the love of God.

Contact: jonathan@gotoheavennow.com
www.gotoheavennow.com